FOOTPRINTS

FOOTPRINTS

Canadian Sports Stories: Summer

By Dave Toms

McArthur & Company

Toronto

First published in Canada in 2004 by
McArthur & Company
322 King St. West, Suite 402
Toronto, Ontario
M5V 1J2
www.mcarthur-co.com

National Library of Canada Cataloguing in Publication

Toms, Dave
Footprints : Canadian sports stories / Dave Toms.

ISBN 1-55278-427-4

1. Athletes—Canada—Biography. 2. Sports—Canada—History.
I. Title.

GV697.A1T64 2004   796'.092'271   C2003-907486-2

Cover & Photo f/x: Rocco Baviera
Composition: Colleen O'Hara/Four Eyes Art + Design

Cover Photo Permissions:
© Canadian Sports Hall of Fame: Bobbie Rosenfeld, Coach Percy Page & the
Edmonton Grads, Ethel Catherwood, Marilyn Bell, Russ Jackson, Mark
Tewksbury, Sylvie Bernier, Ferguson Jenkins, Tom Longboat, The *Bluenose*,
Percy Williams.
© Canpress: Ben Johnson

Printed in Canada by Webcom Limited

The publisher would like to acknowledge the financial support of the Government
of Canada through the Book Publishing Industry Development Program, the Canada
Council for the Arts, and the Ontario Arts Council for our publishing activities.
We also acknowledge the Government of Ontario through the Ontario Media
Development Corporation Ontario Book Initiative.

10 9 8 7 6 5 4 3 2 1

To Scott Young, a great writer and a true friend,
with much love and affection.

D.T.

Thanks for all the times
you've been there for
me . . .

Love

xoxo

❧ CONTENTS ❧

1 /
Ned Hanlan, *Rower* 1
2 /
Bobby Kerr, *Sprinter* 5
3 /
Tommy Burns, *Heavyweight champion of the world* 9
4 /
Tom Longboat, *Distance runner* 13
5 /
The Matchless Six, *Athletics* 19
6 /
George S. Lyon, *Golf* 23
7 /
William Torchy Peden, *Cycling* .27
8 /
Hilda Strike, *Sprinter* 31
9 /
"Peerless" Percy Williams, *Sprinter* 35
10 /
The *Bluenose*, *Fishing schooner* .39
11 /
The Edmonton Grads, *Basketball* 43
12 /
Ethel Catherwood, *High jumper* 47
13 /
Ada Mackenzie, *Golf* 51

❦ CONTENTS ❧

14 /
Normie Kwong, *Football* 55

15 /
Fanny Bobbie Rosenfeld, *All around* 59

16 /
Miss Supertest, Unlimited class powerboat 63

17 /
Marilyn Bell, *Distance swimmer* 67

18 /
George Knudson, *Golf* 71

19 /
Russ Jackson, *Football* 75

20 /
Northern Dancer, *Thoroughbred horse racing* 79

21 /
Harry Jerome, *Sprinter* 83

22 /
Fergie Jenkins, *Baseball* 87

23 /
Jocelyn Lovell, *Cycling* 91

24 /
Gary Beck, *Top Fuel drag racing* 95

25 /
Sylvie Bernier, *Diving* 99

26 /
Debbie Brill, *High jump* 103

❧ CONTENTS ❧

27 /
Diane Jones-Konihowski, *Pentathlon* 107
28 /
The 1976 Montreal Summer Olympic Games 111
29 /
Arnie Boldt, *High jumper* 115
30 /
Terry Fox, *Runner* 119
31 /
Victor Davis, *Swimming* 123
32 /
Sylvie Fréchette, *Synchro swimming* 127
33 /
Lennox Lewis, *Boxing* 131
34 /
Ben Johnson, *Sprinter* 135
35 /
Mark McKoy, *Hurdles* 139
36 /
Curt Harnett, *Cycling* 143
37 /
Mark Tewksbury, *Swimming* .147
38 /
Donny Lalonde, *Light heavyweight
champion of the world* 151

❧ CONTENTS ❧

39 /
Larry Walker, *Baseball* 155

40 /
Caroline Brunet, *Sprint kayak* 159

41 /
Daniel Igali, *Wrestling* 163

42 /
Clara Hughes, *Cycling and long-track speed skating* 167

43 /
Donovan Bailey, *Sprinter* 171

44 /
Silken Laumann, *Rowing* 175

45 /
Kathleen Heddle and Marnie McBean, *Rowing* 179

46 /
Lori Kane, *Golf* 183

47 /
Simon Whitfield, *Triathlon* 187

48 /
Atlanta 4 × 100 Relay Team 191

49 /
Eric Gagné, *Baseball* 195

50 /
Perdita Felicien, *Hurdler* 201

1

Ned Hanlan
Rower

———∞∞∞———

Hometown: Toronto

NED HANLAN WAS BORN IN 1855 — TWELVE YEARS BEFORE Canada became a country. He developed great rowing skills that took him around the world and he became our brand-new country's first international star. To many people from many lands, Ned was the prototype of the new Canadian.

Ned grew up with a paddle in is hand. His parents ran a hotel on Toronto Island and Ned had to cross the harbour daily in all kinds of weather to go to school on the mainland. Some say Ned's dad may have done a little midnight booze smuggling and that Ned might have learned to paddle well at night too. Either way, any fears Ned had of being on the water left him early.

As a teenager, Ned amused himself by entering local regattas in the summer. He won races from the Eastern Beaches all the way down the Lake Ontario shoreline to Port Credit. At 16, his reputation as a paddler was growing.

Ned didn't try his luck rowing a shell until his 18th summer. But Ned took to it right away. He loved the fact that he could generate so much speed. That very summer in 1874 he won the Toronto Amateur Sculling Championships. The trophy sat proudly on the mantel at the hotel.

The promoters swooped in and Ned took a manager to look after the prize money. In those days, rowing and gambling were tough to separate.

In 1876 Ned travelled to Philadelphia to meet 15 of the world's best rowers at the Centennial Regatta. The 21 year old was unknown on the east coast rowing scene, but he set a new world record for the single sculls over a three-mile course and came home to a torchlight parade on the island. Sports fans loved torchlight parades.

After young Ned became the 1878 Canadian Champion in single sculls, he travelled to the Allegheny River for the U.S. Championship Regatta. Ned won easily to establish himself as the best rower in North America. As Ned's reputation grew, so did the prize money. He cast his gaze toward Europe and a bigger audience.

On Britain's Tyne River the following year, Ned met the champion of all England, William Elliot, and crushed him by over 11 lengths. Canada was on the world rowing map and Ned was a presence on any course anywhere.

The year 1880 was the season of dreams for Ned and his fans. He didn't lose a single race all year and constantly played to the crowd. Ned would often sprint ahead of the field then relax, wave to the crowd, sponge off his brow and wait for them to catch up before sprinting ahead once again. He always put on a show.

Most of the English news writers of the day found his antics to be a bit immature. But Ned didn't give a damn what English news writers thought. He was there because he loved the excitement and the crowd. He loved the race. Sometimes Ned stopped to talk during races. Then he'd excuse himself and sprint off to regain the lead, laughing at the other rowers as he glided past, powerful and relentless. Ned got every ounce of energy out of every stroke and yet he seemed to be barely working while other athletes struggled under the task.

Ned's rowing style was revolutionary and he was one of the first rowers to master the new sliding seat. At just 5 feet 5 inches and 155 pounds, Ned developed a long, finished stroke with a strong catch that seemed to lift his scull right out of the water. But even that magic stroke wasn't enough to make him the favourite in the race of the century against world champion E.A. Tricket of Australia on London's Thames River in the fall of Ned's magic year. Tricket stood 6 feet 4 inches tall and outweighed Ned by some 60 pounds. The Canadian in the blue jersey was a big underdog. It couldn't get any better than that for Ned.

The race took place on the famous Thames course where Oxford and Cambridge race every year. The course covers 4 miles, 440 yards. Tricket couldn't shake Ned and the Canadian "boy in blue" took the Australian's world title by three boat lengths. The betting crowd made a fortune that day. So did Ned.

The new World Champion successfully defended his title six times over the next three years, beating back every challenger with ease. He travelled extensively, lived well and rowed in dozens of exhibitions, losing only once. That was to a friend in Toronto after spending some time toasting one another.

In 1884 Ned travelled to the West Coast and then on to Honolulu, Hawaii, for an exhibition en route to Australia and a title defence on the Paramatta River. But the boy in blue lost his luck in the Australian heat and William Beach won the crown back for Australia. Canada would not reclaim the title until 1896 when Jake Gaudaur won it back.

Ned raced seriously into the late 1880s and for fun well into the 1890s. In all, he logged more than three hundred professional wins through his career. Ned lived on the island throughout his life. In 1898 he was elected alderman for Ward 4 and served two terms on Toronto City Council.

Ned Hanlan died in Toronto in January 1908. Hanlan's Point on Toronto's lakeshore bears his name.

2

Bobby Kerr
Sprinter

Hometown: Hamilton

BOBBY WAS A YOUNG CHILD WHEN HIS PARENTS, GEORGE and Rebecca, emigrated from Enniskillen, Ireland, where Bobby was born in 1882. One of a large family, the boy carried traditional Irish pride in the fine sport of foot racing. He was blessed with natural speed and developed good instincts for the art of the race. Thanks to his parents, he grew up with a great respect for the virtues and rewards of hard work. For the Kerrs, life was difficult and times were uncertain. But Bobby gave them hope.

Bobby was already a local star when the Coronation Games were held in Hamilton in the summer of 1902. By the time they were over he was a force on the national scene. Bobby captured three events in the biggest meet of the season — the 100-, 440- and 880-yard races. Once word reached around the country, Bobby was a working-class hero.

The following year Bobby won the 100- and 200-yard events at the YMCA Championships. The victories convinced him to work even harder and he set his sights on the 1904 Olympic track meet in St. Louis. The third Games ever were held in conjunction with the St. Louis World Fair.

Events were spread out over the entire summer and because of the high costs of sending teams only 13 countries attended. Of the 687 athletes who did compete, more than 500 were American. Fifty Canadians made the trip.

Underscoring the timelessness of the plight of amateur sports in Canada is the fact that, in order to get to Missouri, Bobby had to pay his own way. He saved every cent he could from his job as a Hamilton firefighter and then travelled by train to St. Louis and, in order to conserve his cash, arrived just before the event. That cut down his hotel and food budget considerably, but it also left him little time to recuperate from the economy-class train trip. Bobby won a heat in the 100 yards but was eliminated by the eventual winner, Archie Hahn.

The 100- and 200-metre races in St. Louis had identical top three finishes. Archie Hahn won gold, Nathaniel Cartmell took silver and William Hogenson captured bronze. It was a USA sweep and no one was surprised. Bobby, however, was determined to put Canada at the top of the sprint leaderboard.

Once he was back in Hamilton, Bobby shifted gears again. He began to race as often as possible. He vowed to never fall victim to fatigue again. Then he began to reel off the victories and set new Canadian records in every sprint distance imaginable. He held national records at 40, 60, 100 and 220 yards as well as in the 100- and 200-metre distances. Many torchlight parades were held to honour Bobby's triumphant returns home in those days as he reeled off 39 straight races over the next few seasons.

In 1908 Bobby fixed his gaze on London and the Olympics. To get there he swept first the Ontario and then the Canadian Championships. The latter meet served as the Olympic team trials. This time Bobby had better financing. He made the transatlantic voyage with a handful of other members of Canada's team in relative comfort. Where the train trip to St. Louis had been an ordeal, the voyage was a tonic. Bobby arrived in England ready to race.

The London Summer Games revived the flagging Olympic movement. In Paris in 1900 and St. Louis in 1904 the competitions had become sidebars to those cities' World Fair celebrations. In London they stood on their own and attracted more than 2000 athletes from 22 nations.

Once in England, it was determined by Canadian team officials that Bobby would run in both the 100- and 200-metre races in spite of the gruelling pace he'd have to handle. In the space of a day and a half he won his 200-metre semifinal in the morning, placed third and captured bronze in the 100-metre final in the afternoon, then woke up the next morning, had breakfast and captured gold in the 200-metre final. In less than 48 hours Bobby became Canada's first sprint hero of the modern era and our first multimedal Olympic champion. Bobby put his country on the leaderboard.

Bobby's track heroics played big with the London press, who looked upon any son of the British Empire as a son of their own. He was proclaimed in giant headlines as the "Greatest Sprinter in the World." He arrived back home in Hamilton in August and they held the grandest torch parade anyone had ever seen. The Irish community was ecstatic.

In 1909 Bobby went back to his birth country to win the Ireland Championships in the 100- and 200-yard races. He followed that up with victories over the same distances at the British Championships. He held the Canadian titles from 1905 until 1910 when, after winning 400 races, Bobby Kerr retired from competition.

Bobby went on to coach and serve as secretary for both the Hamilton Amateur Athletic Association and the Hamilton Tiger Cats Football Club. He went to the 1928 Amsterdam Olympics and to the 1932 Los Angeles Olympics as a manager of the track and field team and served with the Canadian Olympic Association in many capacities throughout the remainder of his life.

Bobby died in 1963 at the age of 81.

3

Tommy Burns
Heavyweight champion of the world

———⚬⚬⚬———

Hometown: Vancouver

TOMMY BURNS WAS 5 FEET 7 INCHES TALL AND WEIGHED, at his heaviest, 175 pounds — not exactly a huge man. But in 1906 Burns became the Heavyweight Boxing Champion of the world and over the next 34-month period successfully defended his title 11 times.

Burns was born Noah Brusso on June 17, 1881, in Hanover, Ontario. He was one of 13 children in an Italian family trying to make a better life in the new world. He learned how to fight early in life, first with his siblings, and then with his friends, and finally with his rivals. The boy wanted to take lessons and learn how to box properly but was unable to overcome his deeply religious mother's protests and the family's poverty.

His mother's opposition came when he nearly killed an opponent and he changed his name as a result. He crossed the Detroit River and started to fight in Michigan. Then he ran off an impressive string of eight straight knockouts in Detroit to start his career in the ring.

On December 8, 1902, young Brusso fought a three-round exhibition with the legendary Gentlemen Jim Corbett at the packed Detroit Athletic Club. The scrappy Canadian held his own against the former champions and the bout was declared a draw. He was so pumped by the experience that he won the Michigan State Middleweight title nearly three weeks later by knocking out Tom McCune in the seventh round.

In 1903 Noah Brusso fought 12 times and recorded 7 knockouts, making himself a favourite in the Detroit Italian community. In January of 1904 he met Ben O'Grady in Detroit and nearly killed him with a devastating right hand. So he decided to end Noah Brusso's career. He changed his name and travelled west.

Fighting first as Ed Burns and then as Tommy Burns, the boxer rolled through five straight wins in the U.S. Midwest in 1904. Then curiosity took him to the Klondike and an inspection tour of a mine he won in a poker game. When Tommy wasn't fighting or training, he liked to play poker and gamble. While in the Far North he fought the storied Klondike Mike Mahoney to a draw. Mahoney was much bigger than Burns but Tommy could fight. He decided to sell the mine and make his way to the West Coast in search of a big title.

Fighting mostly as a middleweight and occasionally as a heavyweight, Tommy fared well and worked his way into contention for a world title shot. But as he grew older he was finding it difficult to keep his weight down to the middleweight limit. In early 1906, it was announced that Tommy Burns would sign to fight in Los Angeles for the World Middleweight Championship. The weight limit would be 158 pounds.

A month later Tommy changed direction and signed to

fight Marvin Hart for the Heavyweight title instead. The prize money was too much to turn down. Hart was an overwhelming 17 to 1 favourite, but the Canadian pounded out a 20-round (18 out of 20) decision and walked away with the Heavyweight Champion of the World title belt.

Burns took his title on tour and defended it successfully in San Diego, Philadelphia, London, Dublin and Paris. He reasoned the World Champion ought to take the title out into the world and expose as many fans as possible. In return, the fans cheered him on. Tommy's final of three battles against Philadelphia Jack O'Brien still stands as one of the most memorable title fights of all time. Burns won a hard-fought and bloody 20-round decision.

Tommy Burns loved to travel and loved even more to show off his title belt. Late in 1907, he decided to take his championship to Europe and see the sights.

By the summer of 1908 Burns grew bored once again. He'd already defended his belt five times by June — four of the wins came by knockout. Decent challengers were hard to find. Then Tommy's wanderlust called out again and he boarded a liner bound for Australia and new adventures.

Once in Sydney, Burns set out to replenish his bank accounts and fought twice in just eight days, knocking out both of Australia's top heavyweights, Bill Squires and Bill Lang. Shortly after the second fight, Burns came down with what may have been jaundice. He was too weak to fight again until December. That fight became a part of boxing history.

On Christmas Day in 1908 Tommy Burns did something that no other champion in any weight division would do. He gave American Jack Johnson a shot at the title.

Because Johnson was black no one would risk losing his belt to him. Racism was common and accepted. But Tommy saw things differently and in spite of his subpar physical condition he agreed to fight Johnson. They met at Rushcutters Bay in Sydney. Johnson towered over Burns and was soon in control. Burns, though, wouldn't concede a millimetre. After 14 rounds, the local police had seen enough blood and they stepped in to stop the fight. Jack Johnson became the Heavyweight Champion of the World — the first black boxer to hold a belt in any division. Tommy was thoroughly beaten.

Four months after losing the belt, Burns won a rematch with the Australian Bill Lang and claimed the British Heavyweight Championship. He fought on until he was nearly 40 and then retired after 62 professional bouts.

Burns died penniless in Vancouver in 1955. There were only four people at his funeral. In 1961 the city finally placed a marker on his numbered grave, using money donated by the Canadian Olympic boxing fund.

Tom Longboat
Distance runner

Hometown: Six Nations, Ontario

IN HIS LAST YEARS ON EARTH, TOM LONGBOAT WENT home to the bush and the humble log cabin where he was born on the Six Nations Reserve in Southwestern Ontario. Tom, an Onondaga and a member of the Iroquois Confederacy, spent his final summer on the porch there watching the Grand River flow past the land where he learned how to run as a child.

Tom's dad died tragically when Tom was a young boy, leaving his mom all alone to raise four children. The boys often walked to Brantford — 15 miles each way. Tom grew strong. At 10 he ran a neighbour's cow into exhaustion. The owner of the cow wasn't amused by his antics, but he sure had some respect for Tom's determination. By 18 Tom was the best distance runner in all the Six Nations.

At 19 Tom ventured away from his home turf and entered the Around the Bay Race in Hamilton. It was his first-ever marathon. He won. Ten days later he rolled to victory in Toronto's Ward Race. The press was less than kind and many writers made derisive comments about Tom's heritage. One said he looked ridiculous in his old bathing suit. Another said his hair looked like it had been cut with a tomahawk. But the gamblers who bet on Tom won big. He laughed off the negative comments and began his ascent.

In April 1907 Longboat won the Boston Marathon — the most prestigious race in the Americas — and smashed the course record by five and a half minutes. When news flashed home on the wire, he became an instant celebrity. Toronto was hungry for celebrity. The city threw a big parade for Longboat, but he felt little real respect from Mayor Emerson Coatsworth or any of the dignitaries, and the ongoing racist remarks in the newspapers wounded him deeply.

Tom joined the Irish-Canadian Athletic Club and contracted with a new manager, Tom Flanagan. The manager found it amusing to install his star runner as a cigar store proprietor so that Tom's amateur status could be maintained. That way, Tom would go to London's Summer Olympics in 1908 as the heavy favourite for marathon gold. Big odds always attract big gambling money.

While running in apparent comfort in second place during the Olympic marathon, Tom collapsed. He was at the 19-mile marker when he went down. Longboat was carried from the course on a stretcher — convulsing and protesting that he'd been poisoned. J. Howard Crocker, manager of the Canadian team, later alleged in his official report that strychnine poisoning was the probable cause of Tom's demise in the race. That drug was a common stimulant in the day and popular with marathoners, but only in the right amount. Speculation arose that Tom had been administered the wrong amount. His Olympic Games were over.

Further down the course, Dorando Pietri of Italy entered the stadium to a roar from the crowd. But he too collapsed, short of the finish line. Then an extraordinary thing happened: in the excitement, a trackside official forgot himself and shouted encouragement to the crumpling winner. Dorando Pietri was, of course, immediately disqualified and John Hayes of the USA took the Olympic marathon crown. The "helping" official turned out to be Sir Arthur Conan Doyle, the creator of the world's most famous detective, Sherlock Holmes.

Canadians were shocked at the transatlantic cable news of Tom's misfortune. Rumours ran rampant that Flanagan had deliberately poisoned his runner after betting against him and cleaning up on the long odds. Tom left England and came home to heal. No further investigation was launched. Crocker's report was buried away in a file somewhere and the story died.

Tom turned professional and took the train to New York City with Flanagan and *Toronto Daily Star* sportswriter Lou Marsh. He would take part in the match-race series against the two main event runners from London: the Olympic champion John Hayes and the crowd-pleasing Italian star Dorando Pietri. The races would be held indoors at Madison Square Garden. Tom dominated the series and became the runner of the age in the eyes of American fans.

While in New York, Tom met and fell in love with Lauretta Maracle — a Mohawk from the Bay of Quinte on Lake Ontario. They were married in a ceremony at Massey Hall on December 15, 1908, before a theatre filled with well-wishers. The *Globe* described Lauretta as looking "more white than Indian." Tom tried to smile and pretend it didn't hurt.

Longboat and Flanagan began to fight over where the money was going. Lauretta angered her husband's manager by pushing for more financial accountability and more say in how expenses were handled. Tom had never paid much attention to money. He just liked having a fat bankroll in his pocket. After a rematch with Dorando in Buffalo, which Tom won, Flanagan sold Tom's contract to a New York promoter. It humiliated Tom to be sold like livestock. He went to Manhattan with a very heavy heart.

Tom found it more and more difficult to train, but he entered into a memorable series with British Champion Alf Shrubb that lasted over the next few years. Tom won more than he lost and made plenty of money through the period. The Longboats lived very comfortably.

In his final big contest on February 5, 1912, he set a 15-mile record in Edinburgh, Scotland. But Tom had had enough of living in the spotlight and tried to settle down. Family, friends and bad investments soon devoured the money that Lauretta had saved for their future. War in Europe, however, had turned the big crowds into trickles and the money in Tom's sport had dried up. He couldn't go back to the track. He'd fight for his country instead.

Tom enlisted and served in World War I with the vaunted 180th Sportsmen's Battalion, alongside Conn Smythe who would later own the Toronto Maple Leafs. Tom ran races for the unit at local events around Ontario while recruiters made their enlistment pitch. The army would need thousands of young Canadian men.

When the battalion shipped overseas, Tom naturally

became a courier. His job was to run correspondence from company headquarters to the battlefield. At Ypres he was caught by enemy artillery fire and reported dead. Although he was badly wounded, he had in fact survived. The mistaken report was never corrected, however, and when Tom went home in 1919 to Lauretta — shock. Believing him to be dead, she had remarried. He headed for the bush.

With the money from his career gone, Tom took a job with the City of Toronto as a garbage collector. In 1935 the press hammered him as a drunken Indian after he was charged with driving under the influence (DUI). At the same time, an imposter posing as Tom was hitting up beerhall patrons in the West End of the city for free drinks.

People turned their backs on the proud man. Tom tried to get on with his life and he remarried. He tried to pass on his mother's dignity and his own grit to his four children.

Tom Longboat died at home in January 1949. His funeral took place in the longhouse and cars filled the streets and lawns. People spilled outside the building as the elders, singers and dancers helped set Tom's spirit free to join his ancestors.

5

The Matchless Six
Athletics

IN 1896 THE FRENCH ARISTOCRAT PIERRE DE COUBERTIN realized a lifelong dream when the first Olympic Games of the modern era were held in Athens. However, when the best of our youth gathered to compete for rare Olympic medals, only the men were allowed to play. Although women were allowed to take part in artistic demonstrations, they were banned from competing as full medal athletes. It took three decades for the International Olympic Committee to begin to address the inequity of their Olympic program and start to make it a modern event.

The Summer Olympics of Amsterdam in 1928 were mandated to include women's swimming and athletics events for the first time. The events would have full medal status but the whole experience would be considered experimental. The final decision to include women on a full-time basis would be made sometime after the closing ceremony. Individual national organizing committees were advised to assemble teams of women to compete for their respective countries. Separate points standings would be kept, declaring overall winners in both men's and women's events. It was up to individual countries to decide whether or not to participate.

The debate in Canada was heated. One side argued that women should be equal in every way to men. The other side said that rigorous competition would be detrimental to women's physical well-being. Some even suggested that it would impede the ability of participants to conceive and deliver babies. One member of this was sportsman A.S. Lamb. Fortunately, Canadian officials decided against his group and elected to send a team of women to Amsterdam to represent Canada. Unfortunately, Lamb was the manager of Canada's team.

The call went out across Canada and six women emerged from various Canadian championships to win the right to form Canada's first Olympic athletics team. Fanny Bobbie Rosenfeld, Myrtle Cook, Jane Bell, Ethel Catherwood, Jean Thompson and Ethel Smith were immediately dubbed the "Marvellous Six" by the press. The name changed later.

The women would compete in only five athletic events: the 100-metre sprint, the 800-metre run, the high jump, the discus and the 4 × 100-metre relay. The 16-member team from the USA was expected to win the meet. At least, that's how the American sportswriters saw it.

Canada looked good in the 100-metre sprint. A sweep was not out of the question. Myrtle Cook set a new world record at the Canadian championships when she narrowly beat out Bobbie Rosenfeld, who was right on form. The two Torontonians were used to pushing each other hard during races. Ethel Smith was the third member of the team in the race and she had a shot too.

Bad luck or a bad starter knocked Cook out of contention after two false starts. Her intensity and desire to win caused her disqualification. She sat beside the track sobbing while the others dug in. Rosenfeld and Smith would have to carry on for Canada.

The 100-metre race finished in a dead heat with Bobbie Rosenfeld and Betty Thompson of the USA clocking identical times on the four officials' stopwatches. Lamb was on the scene representing Canada. He conceded on behalf of the Canadian runner in the name of good sportsmanship. The Americans got the gold. Ethel Smith won bronze.

Nineteen-year-old Ethel Catherwood won at the high jump when she cleared 1.59 metres. Her gold medal is still the only Canadian victory in individual Olympic women's track and field event competition. In a hastily arranged Olympic beauty pageant, Ethel was named the most beautiful girl at the Games and called the "Saskatoon Lily" by writers of the day. The Olympic movement still had a long way to go.

The 800-metre race became the single most important race of the meet for Canada. Even though no medal was won, Bobbie Rosenfeld stepped up to fuse the team's spirit. She sacrificed her own position in the race to encourage her struggling and injured teammate Jean Thompson to go on. When they crossed the finish line, the other members of the team mobbed them. After that moment, Canada's women were invincible.

In the 4 x 100-metre relay it came down to winner take all. Canada and the USA were in a battle for team honours and the winner of the relay would win the crown. It wasn't even close. Rosenfeld ran lead-off and gave Ethel Smith a 1-yard gap over the Americans. Smith added another step and passed-off to Jane Bell who held the lead through the third leg. Myrtle Cook was at top speed by the time Bell got into the transition zone for the final baton pass. The Canadian came inches from her second disqualification, but Cook was not going to be denied twice. She ran away from the USA to victory and gold for Canada. The team title belonged to Canada's women. In an instant they became known as the "Matchless Six."

The team returned home through Halifax, Montreal, Ottawa and Toronto. The Olympic entourage included the Matchless Six, Percy Williams, who was the hero for Canada on the men's side with double gold in the sprints, and Torchy Peden. More than 300,000 people jammed Union Station and Front Street in Toronto to greet their heroes. It was the largest crowd in the history of the city, with nearly half the population celebrating in the streets.

After Amsterdam, the International Olympic Committee decided to allow women to compete in the Games. A.S. Lamb voiced his opposition, was ignored and faded into obscurity.

After the Games, Myrtle Cook and Bobbie Rosenfeld became sportswriters for the *Montreal Star* and the Toronto *Globe and Mail*, respectively. They both used their columns and their influence to further the cause of women in sports. Ethel Catherwood and Jean Thompson travelled back to Saskatchewan together and then Ethel moved to the U.S. and drifted out of contact. Jane Bell became a physical education teacher and Ethel Smith settled down to marriage and a family.

The International Olympic Committee still allows countries that ban women from competitive sports in their own countries to compete at the Olympic Games.

George S. Lyon
Golf

Hometown: Toronto

GEORGE LYON WAS 38 YEARS OLD BEFORE HE EVER PICKED up a golf club. He had already served as a member of the Queen's Own Rifles in the Métis uprising on the Prairies in 1885. He was already a local hero on the Toronto sports scene for setting a Canadian record in the pole vault. He played baseball all summer and was in the books for scoring 234 runs without an out in an 1894 cricket match, a world record that stood for 40 years. But at an age when most athletes think about retirement, George was about to become a rookie and a champion.

Cricket was George's first love, but he loved the very concept of a challenge nearly as much. So when a neighbour challenged him to see if he could hit a golf ball as hard as he could in cricket, he accepted. He hopped the fence around the Rosedale Golf Course, stepped up to the tee, addressed the ball and took a swing. Like a lot of golf beginners, George was hooked.

George had a faster learning curve than most. He was abundantly blessed with natural athletic ability. In 1898, after just three seasons playing the game, he became the Canadian Amateur Champion. He won that title seven more times through his late-blooming career on the golf course.

George had a strange swing, no doubt shaped by his years on the cricket pitch. He relied on the power of his large arms and wrists rather than on a fluid stroke, but he kept perfectly balanced right through the unorthodox swing. And he had plenty of power and accuracy to his shots, especially with his irons. An American writer described him as "a man cutting wheat with a scythe." George just laughed it off, pulled out a club and cut down his next opponent.

In 1904 the International Olympic Committee staged the Summer Games in St. Louis, Missouri. They would coincide with the St. Louis World's Fair. For the first and only time, the IOC decided to include golf on the schedule of full medal Olympic events. George loved the ideals of the Olympic movement and decided to represent Canada in Missouri in the summer.

Eighty-seven golfers took part in a qualifying round, and the top 32 best scores advanced to the Olympic tournament. Then competitors played an elimination-match format. One loss meant elimination. The gold medal match would feature the two undefeated survivors of the head-to-head rounds.

Nobody gave the 48 year old from Canada much of a chance. But George loved the environment and became stimulated by the quest. He thrived on the match-play format and set a new course record on his way to the final showdown. Incredibly, he was growing stronger as the days passed. His opponent for the gold medal was Chandler Egan, the U.S. Amateur Champion. Egan was an overwhelming favourite for the home crowd in St. Louis. He was also 20 years old — less than half George's age. But that didn't mean a thing.

In the gold-medal final, the golfers would play a round in the morning, have lunch and then play another 18 holes if necessary in the afternoon. The man who was up by the most holes would win the Olympic crown. Clean and simple.

At the 18-hole turnaround, George Lyon of Canada was up by one and going strong. He kept up a running dialogue and joked with the fans throughout the match, as usual. Egan, on the other hand, was growing more withdrawn. The young American appeared to be tiring from the demands of the long tourney, and his game was coming undone. He never got the chance to turn it around.

On the second hole of the final round, Egan pushed his drive into the rough, and then on the next tee he buried himself behind a tree. He was scrambling. George's "man-cutting-wheat swing" was true and straight. The crowd could feel an upset in the making.

By the time the golfers reached the 16th tee, George was ahead by two strokes. The young American champion sliced his drive into a tough spot at the edge of a water hazard. George drove straight down the fairway. Egan never recovered and Lyon won the hole to go up by three and seal the match. George was pleased.

Canada recorded a gold medal and George was given the title of world's best golfer. At the awards ceremony back at the clubhouse, George pulled out an old trick and walked to the presentation on his hands. All 48 years of him. The crowd roared in approval. George was presented with a trophy and he stands as the only gold-medal Olympic golfer of all time.

In 1908 when London team officials couldn't settle on a format for a golf tournament, the International Olympic Committee dropped the sport from competition. It has never been revived, although the subject comes up from time to time.

At home, George was at the forefront of an explosion in golf's popularity. Many Canadians reasoned that if George at 48 could win Olympic gold, they too could probably find some satisfaction in the game.

George kept playing throughout his life and realized the great ambition of many avid golfers by scoring in the 70s while he was in his seventies. At 76 he recorded a hole in one. Lyon died in 1938 just shy of his 80th birthday. Over time, his family lost track of his Olympic medal, so in 2000 the IOC had a new one minted just for them.

7

William Torchy Peden
Cycling

Hometown: Victoria

IN 1926 A VICTORIA SPORTSWRITER DESCRIBED WILLIAM Peden this way: "The flame-haired Victoria youth led the pack like a torch." The nickname "Torchy" stuck like glue from that day on.

Torchy was a local hero and all-round sports star. He was nationally ranked as a swimmer and as a cyclist. When he could no longer accommodate the demands of both sports he made the decision to ride and became the grandfather of Canadian cycling.

Torchy travelled to Amsterdam in 1928 as a member of Canada's greatest Olympic team ever. The fourth-place finish in the final standings that they posted has never been equalled. Canada's Olympic team was loaded with heroes, including double gold-medal sprinter Percy Williams and the first-ever women's Olympic team, the Matchless Six — Fanny Bobbie Rosenfeld, Myrtle Cook, Ethel Smith, Jane Bell, Jean Thompson and Ethel Catherwood. Torchy was expected to be on the list of podium-bound athletes. But he only attended medal ceremonies for teammates in the Netherlands.

Torchy always regretted that he didn't add to Canada's

medal haul in the summer of 1928, but he came down with food poisoning just before the race and then suffered through three flat tires out on the course. The big redhead was too disappointed and maybe too embarrassed to return home right away. He decided to stay on to race in Europe for a while. He found his destiny on the tracks there.

Torchy turned pro after Amsterdam and then, after scouting out the cycling scene in Europe, made the journey home to Victoria to enlist his younger brother, Doug, as his six-day race partner. Six-day races were becoming big events on both sides of the Atlantic for fans, for gamblers and for big-time promoters. Over the next few seasons Torchy and Doug became one of the most popular teams on the European circuits and in the growing North American market.

Six-day races were gruelling affairs that saw teams of two ride in shifts around the clock and around the track — lap after lap for six straight days. The races could be staged indoors or out and were held year-round. The Peden brothers from Victoria were masters of the art. By the early 1930s cycling events were as big as any sport in America. The races often drew more fans than baseball. An event in New Jersey at the Nutley Velodrome drew nearly 300,000 spectators. Many of them were fans of the wild Canadian redhead, Torchy Peden.

The sport was even more popular indoors — especially in the bad-weather months — and fans jammed the big-city arenas to watch the drama of races unfold. One of the biggest events of the sports season in New York was the Madison Race held annually at Madison Square Garden. Maple Leaf Gardens and the Montreal Forum also became stops on the six-day tour. When Torchy appeared at Canadian races he was mobbed.

The biggest race promoters of the day were the metropolitan newspapers. They invested in and created events that were specifically designed to sell their editions throughout the day. The morning edition might have entirely different standings to publish than the one in the evening. In this environment, with newspaper hawkers calling out his name, Torchy became a star. He was one of just a handful of riders who could command and get the magic $1000-a-day fee.

Torchy made up to $20,000 a year at the height of his career and at the height of the Great Depression, a sum that easily afforded him anything he wanted. He lived well, took care of his family and invested wherever he was able. Mostly, though, he just wanted to race.

His popularity was so great that Torchy received a gold-plated bicycle from his main sponsor CCM — Canadian Cycle and Motor Company. He rode the gilded bike at exhibitions around Canada, which delighted both the manufacturer and the small-town crowds who flocked to see this great celebrity in their midst.

Torchy earned the accolades and the rewards that came his way by performing on the track where it counted. In 1931 he set the 1-mile world record. Then on a brand-new velodrome in the Beaches area of Toronto he set a new world speed record, travelling nearly 120 kilometres per hour. In 1934 he was singled out by the sports press and named the best long-distance racer in the world. The sport of cycling belonged to Torchy.

But by the late thirties the circuit was drying up. The

Depression had taken a big toll on its fan base and cars were becoming everyone's favourite race vehicle. They were louder and much more spectacular than bikes, especially the crashes.

Torchy rode on through those tough years and then enlisted when World War II broke out in Europe. He resumed his career after the war, but interest in racing had dried up in North America and the sport was rebuilding in Europe. There was nowhere left to ride.

Torchy retired with a Hall of Fame record. In all, he started 148 races and finished 145. He won 38 times against the best in the world, a record that stood until 1965, and was one of the most popular athletes of his era.

He died in Victoria on January 26, 1980.

Hilda Strike
Sprinter

⸺◦⸺

Hometown: Montreal

HILDA STRIKE WAS DISCOVERED PLAYING SOFTBALL ON A field in Montreal by 1928 Olympic star runner Myrtle Cook. Myrtle was one of the Matchless Six — Canada's first-ever women's team for the Amsterdam Summer Games that year. After retiring, Myrtle moved to Montreal, where she wrote a sports column. When Hilda ran out a ground ball, Myrtle's eyes opened wide. She recognized world-class speed when she saw it.

Under Myrtle's guiding hand, Hilda became the best sprinter of her era. From 1929 until 1932 she was unbeatable as a sprinter and was widely recognized in the world of track and field as the fastest woman alive. As such, Hilda became the overwhelming favourite to win the 100-metre gold medal at the 1932 Summer Olympics in Los Angeles. She travelled west filled with expectation.

Hosting the Olympics in Los Angeles posed economic problems for many countries. The sports organizations simply didn't have the funds to send athletes all that way. So the International Olympic Committee expanded the rules to allow American athletes with European roots to compete for the foreign team. For the most part, it was a wise solution.

31

The whole world could compete that way.

The 100-metre final was held at the brand-new L.A. Coliseum. The spectacular columned stadium was the central showpiece of the Games. It turned out to be one of the greatest Olympic sprint finals of all time and one of the most controversial. Hilda had to fight with everything she had in order to catch the previously unknown Polish runner, fast-breaking Stanislawa Walasiewicz. Both runners hit the finish line with identical times of 11.9 seconds. Willy von Bremen of the USA was third in 12.0, less than a heartbeat behind.

The officials checked their stopwatches and conferred on the infield — it was decades before digital timing — then they awarded the gold medal to the Polish sprinter and the silver to Hilda. Hilda stood dazed.

Film of the post-race interviews shows Stanislawa speaking perfect high-squeaky-voice English. It was revealed that the Polish gold medallist lived in the USA. She was competing under the new IOC rule as the child of immigrant Poles. She said that she was very happy to win the gold medal for Poland. No one paid much attention to her lack of previous results. It was a feel-good story.

Hilda felt robbed. It was difficult for her to project happiness through such tremendous disappointment. The post-race photo shows a forced smile tightly drawn across her brave face. How had the world's fastest woman run such a great race only to be beaten by an unknown? Myrtle Cook had no answers. Nobody did. Even the winner looks troubled in the shot. It would be decades before Hilda Strike realized just how close to the mark her intuition was at the medal ceremony on that day back in 1932.

The Olympic Games always move forward, and Hilda Strike had to prepare to run with Canada's vaunted relay team in the 4 × 100 final.

The Coliseum crowd was on its feet from the start as a roar of expectancy followed the runners around the cinder track. It all came down to Canada and the USA as, once again, the runners hit the finish line in a dead heat. Both clocked identical times of 47 seconds and set a new Olympic Games record! Great Britain was a distant third.

The officials huddled on the sideline to check their watches as the runners, the press and the whole stadium waited. Finally, the Los Angeles crowd erupted when the gold was awarded to the USA. Strike and Canada's women were left to stand on the silver step of the medal podium.

Hilda went home to Montreal and retired.

Thirty years later in Cleveland the body of Stella Walsh was found shot dead in a seedy motel room. At the Los Angeles Olympics in 1932 Stella Walsh ran for Poland as Stanislawa Walasiewicz. The ensuing autopsy revealed Stella to be a fraud. The women's 100-metre gold medal had been awarded to a man. Stanislawa was, in fact, Stan.

It wasn't until 1968 that the International Olympic Committee made gender testing standard for Olympic athletes. It is interesting to note that several high-ranking international athletes retired just before the Olympics in Mexico City that summer.

Hilda Strike died of natural causes in 1989. Her medal of record in the 100-metre final at the Olympic Games of 1932 is still silver.

"Peerless" Percy Williams

Sprinter

Hometown: Vancouver

PERCY WILLIAMS WAS BORN IN 1908, AN OLYMPIC YEAR — the very same Olympic year that Bobby Kerr of Hamilton established Canada as a sprint nation when he won gold in the 200- and bronze in the 100-metre races in London. Maybe Percy's destiny was already set.

Percy was just a boy when his father left the family, leaving his mom to raise him alone. Young Percy didn't play much with the neighbourhood kids. Sports just didn't hold his interest and neither did running with the pack of boys in his part of town, even though he was the fastest runner in the area.

Thankfully, the lad's natural-born speed did not pass completely unnoticed. Granger saw Percy win against Wally Scott, whom Granger coached, and then he asked him to try out. The coach was also the school janitor and his sports time was strictly on a volunteer basis. No one quite understood why he spent so much time with the reluctant runner. But where most saw a headache, Granger saw a champion in waiting.

The coach was way ahead of his time and looked upon as a bit of an eccentric by his peers. He wrapped his athletes in blankets to keep their muscles warm and limited the number of races they ran to limit the possibility of injury; Percy only ran about a hundred full sprints in his entire career. He also broke the sprint down into component parts to be worked on separately and he used massage to keep his runners relaxed and ready. Things we accept as normal now weren't then. Granger, the outsider, was in fact a great track innovator.

In Percy's first big race he became champion of the Vancouver School District. Granger decided to coach the boy full time and knew that his young protégé would have to go East to prove his speed, a journey that Western athletes know well.

When he won both the 100 and 200 at a qualification meet in Hamilton, heads began to turn his way. Then, in the early summer of 1928 at the Canadian Olympic team trials, he stunned the entire track community by winning the 100 in 10.6 seconds, equalling the Olympic record. He punctuated the meet by cruising to victory in the 200 as well. Percy could flat out fly through the last half of a race. Percy Williams, "The Vancouver Schoolboy," would follow the trail laid by Bobby Kerr back in the year they shared, 1908. He would wear the Red Leaf at the Olympics in Amsterdam later that summer.

Percy met the Canadian team at the docks and boarded for the voyage to Europe. Torchy Peden from Victoria, Ethel Catherwood from Saskatoon, Fanny Bobbie Rosenfeld from Toronto and the other athletes bound for the Games made it a real patriotic trip. The athletes worked out daily on deck to keep fit. While Percy was sailing to Europe in relative comfort with the team, Bob Granger was working his way across the Atlantic as a deckhand on a very smelly cattle boat.

In Amsterdam Percy stayed away from the team and requested his own room. Granger soon moved in so they could work on the sprinter's starts. Granger had no official status with the Canadian delegation. But he was determined to see his sprinter perform at top form. Granger built a workout area right in the room. Percy would take two or thee steps from his set position and then crash into the mattress his coach had propped against the hotel-room wall. But his starts were getting quicker and quicker.

Everything paid off when Percy beat back 84 of the best runners in the world to take the 100-metre sprint in 10.8 seconds. In the final he broke out front with his start and just floated away from the pack. Then Granger and Percy prepared for the 200-metre final. Percy ran it in 21.8 seconds to capture a second gold medal. News reached back to Canada and fans rejoiced at the news of Percy's victory.

Percy's trip back to Vancouver was one dizzying parade from coast to coast. The athletes made stops all along the route to acknowledge their supporters. The women's team (known as the Matchless Six) and Percy were objects of much national affection. The usually reserved Percy revelled in the adulation. At last he seemed happy in a crowd.

Percy followed his glorious Olympic performance with an equally brilliant showing at the British Empire Games in 1930, when he set a new world record in the 100-yard dash. The world press proclaimed him "Peerless Percy," king of the track.

The Williams saga didn't sit well with American track

officials who called Percy's victories in Amsterdam a fluke and said that American Eddie Tolan lost the race to Percy on a technicality. A challenge was issued and Percy, along with Granger, embarked on a gruelling 21-race series against the world's best — the Iron Guts Tour. Percy blew them all away and won 19 of the races, making him the unqualified fastest man alive. The accolades filled Percy up. At just 22 he was on top of the world.

At the end of the challenge series Percy suffered a muscle tear that grew worse throughout the lead-up to the 1932 Los Angeles Olympics. But his love of adulation drove him on. In fact, Percy didn't much like the running part at all. But he desperately wanted to defend his Olympic titles and bathe in the Olympic media spotlight one more time.

The injury was a career-ender though, and Percy pulled up lame in the 100-metre quarterfinals and failed to advance. His Olympic title defence was over. There was no fanfare when he came home this time. Percy never ran again. Nor did he ever stand in front of a large crowd as the hero. He missed that so much.

Percy continued to live with his mother in Vancouver and he became an insurance agent. He made very few public appearances and lived in relative obscurity. In 1977 his mother died and he lived alone. His ongoing battle with alcohol coupled with severe arthritic pain amplified the loneliness he must have felt. In November of 1982 Percy ended his life with a shot from a commemorative starter's pistol he'd been given back in the glory days.

No other Canadian has ever won both the 100- and 200-metre Olympic sprints. A statue in his likeness and in his honour can be found at Vancouver International Airport.

10

The *Bluenose*
Fishing schooner

—❦—

Hometown: Lunenburg, Nova Scotia

DURING THE FIRST DECADES OF THE TWENTIETH CENTURY, the east coast North American ports were vital and bustling fishing centres. Rivalries ran deep, harbour to harbour, through the fleets. But none ran deeper than the one between Lunenburg, Nova Scotia, the home of Maritime Canada's top fleet, and Gloucester, Massachusetts, the pride of New England's great fishery. So in 1920, when the venerable America's Cup was cancelled due to high winds, the announcement sent a ripple of derisive laughter through the ranks of the weather-toughened fishermen on both sides of the border. By their reckoning, true sailors and true boats could handle any kind of weather offered up by Mother Nature.

William H. Dennis, the owner of the *Halifax Herald*, saw the yacht race cancellation and the fleet rivalry as an opportunity, so his newspaper offered up a new prize, the International Fishermen's Trophy. It would be awarded annually to the fastest working schooner in the Atlantic fleet. Only legitimate fishing boats and crews could qualify and they'd race no matter how high the winds. They'd show the yacht club crowd what sea worthiness was all about.

The fleets held elimination races to determine the challengers. At Lunenburg, Captain Thomas Himmelman took his crew to victory aboard the *Delawana*, narrowly edging the *Gilbert B. Walters* under Captain Angus Walters and his proud crew. They faced Gloucester's pride, the *Esperanto*, under Captain Marty Welch in a best-two-of-three series in October of 1920 off the coast of Halifax.

Much to the delight of the Gloucestermen, the debut edition of the Fisherman's International Trophy sailed home aboard the *Esperanto* after two straight wins. In Lunenburg, the locals filled themselves with grim resolve to muster a serious challenge and take the prize back from the Americans.

Local naval architect William J. Roué was commissioned to construct a schooner that would conquer the North Atlantic fishing grounds. He designed and built the 145-footer for $35,000, with the explicit goal of winning back the Canadian fleet's pride. On March 26, 1921, Captain Angus Walters, who'd help raise the money to build her, sailed the *Bluenose* out of Smith & Rhuland Shipyard into Lunenburg's harbour and into history.

Captain Walters and his crew of 32 faced the formidable task of establishing the *Bluenose* as a legitimate member of the fishing fleet. She did Walters and the fleet proud, serving for 21 years through fair and foul weather in a job where most schooners only lasted 10. Over her working career she made it through fierce North Atlantic storms that claimed a great many lives. Walters knew on her maiden voyage that the *Bluenose* was the right ship to represent the fleet at the next set of races for the International Fisherman's Trophy.

Walters and his crew easily beat back the challenge of seven other Canadian schooners to win the right to represent the Maritimes fleet against the *Elsie of Gloucester* under Captain Marty Welch. They met to race in October off of Gloucester on the American boat's home ground. The *Bluenose* flew to victory and swept in two straight races. With the International Fisherman's Trophy safely stowed, the champion of the Lunenburg fleet headed home, flags flying. The entire province of Nova Scotia celebrated the win.

Angus Walters and the *Bluenose* crew never relinquished the trophy again in spite of the many challenges mounted to take it away. The Gloucester fleet could never design and build a boat that was the equal of the *Bluenose*. Her supremacy at sea filled Maritime Canadians with a sense of pride. The men of Lunenburg walked with a swagger in their step.

In the 1930s, with the fleet switching from wind to diesel power, the *Bluenose* became a showboat and toured the Great Lakes. She was also invited to attend the Silver Jubilee of King George V and Queen Mary and crossed the Atlantic to proudly represent Canada at that royal event.

By 1938 war was looming in Europe and interest in sailing dropped off dramatically. The last International Fishermen's Trophy series was held off Gloucester at the end of that fishing season. It was a best-of-five competition pitting the *Bluenose* against long-time rival the *Gertrude L. Thebaud*. The series fittingly came down to the fifth race, and in light winds the *Bluenose* won by more than two minutes. The International Fishermen's Trophy made one final triumphant voyage back to Lunenburg.

Profits from fishing declined and by 1942 Captain Angus Walters could no longer afford to keep up the *Bluenose* and she was sold to the West Indies Trading Company. She served as a Caribbean trader until 1946 when one dark January night she struck a reef off Haiti and, while all hands aboard were saved, the grand champion of sail was lost. The era of wind was officially over.

The *Bluenose* became a visual symbol of Canada's connection to the sea. A likeness of her under full sail still adorns the back of Canada's ten-cent piece. A true-to-the-last-detail replica was built and launched in 1963 and in 1971 was sold to the province of Nova Scotia for one dollar. The *Bluenose II*, like the original, was built at the Smith & Rhuland Shipyard in Lunenburg, Nova Scotia.

11

The Edmonton Grads
Basketball

Hometown: Edmonton

IN 1912 J. ("JOHN") PERCY PAGE LEFT HIS TEACHING position in St. Thomas, Ontario, to accept the challenge of introducing commercial training in the Edmonton high school system. He travelled west by rail to accept his new responsibilities.

Two years later Page formed the first-ever McDougall Commercial High School basketball teams — one for the boys and one for the girls. The sport was relatively new and Page figured it to be the perfect pastime for the Prairie winters. Since he could only coach one team, Percy let his assistant choose a team of preference. The assistant decided to choose the boys' team. John Percy Page got a trip into history.

Page and his players had to fight the popular myth that strenuous sports were harmful to females. Some critics suggested that girls who played boys' sports might do irreparable damage to their reproductive organs. Page thought that was a lot of crap. The team went on to win both the city and the provincial championships. The critics grew silent and the players decided to stay together to compete as adults. The McDougall squad would act as a farm team supplying them with players. The Edmonton Grads were born. There has never been a more successful Canadian team.

By 1923 (the year they won the Canadian championship) the Grads had distinguished themselves as the best in the West. So, when the self-proclaimed world champion Shamrocks from London, Ontario, invited them East to play, Page jumped at the opportunity. The Grads made Percy's trip back to Ontario memorable when they beat the Shamrocks soundly in a two-game total-points series. The Edmonton team went home on the train with the title of Canadian Champions and a trophy to prove it.

Later that year coach Page engineered a lesson in commercial negotiations and signed the Underwood Typewriter Company up as a team sponsor and booster of women's sports. Each year, the Underwood Trophy would go to the best team in North America. The first challenge put the Grads up against the Cleveland Favorite Knits. The U.S. team had the words *World Champs* stamped across their shorts. The Grads were not impressed and beat the Knits in two straight games to take the Underwood. They held on to the trophy for 17 years straight.

Edmonton compiled a 54–6 season that year. Coach Page reminded his girls: "You're ladies first and basketball players second and if you can't win playing a clean game, you don't deserve to win." The more they won together, the more the team relied on him and his philosophy of the game. For 25 seasons, Page held twice-weekly practice and he missed only three times. His core rule was that winning fairly was the only way to win. The Grads kept winning.

In 1924 the Grads were invited to participate in the Paris Olympics exhibition tournament for women. They represented Canada at three more Olympics — Amsterdam in 1928, Los Angeles in 1932 and Berlin in 1936. They won all 27 of their Olympic games and outscored the opposition by a total of 1863 points to 297; however, the women's competition was never a fully recognized Olympic sport, so no medals were awarded. But everyone who knew basketball knew that the Grads were the best team in the world.

In their 17-year domination of the Underwood Trophy, the Grads won 114 games and lost only 6. At one point they strung together 147 straight wins without a single defeat. No team in any sport can lay claim to such a dominant run.

Coach Page and the Grads' record will likely stand for all time — 502 wins against 20 losses. In all, 38 women played for the team throughout its 25-year history.

The team captains through the years were Page favourites and they stayed with the program. Winnie Martin led the team to Paris in 1924. Elsie Benny wore the "C" in 1928 at Amsterdam. Margaret MacBurney, who wore the Grad uniform for 12 years, was captain in 1932 in Los Angeles and Gladys Fry led the squad to Berlin in 1936. The team's leading career scorer was Noel MacDonald, with nearly 2000 points.

In 1940 Percy Page made the difficult decision to disband the team. The advent of Word War II saw crowds drop off and interest in most sports wane. The seriousness of war made games seem foolish. When the British Commonwealth Air Training Plan took over their arena, the Grads had no home. So the gold-and-black uniforms were folded and put away for good.

John Percy Page went on to become a Member of the Legislature for Alberta and served from 1940 to 1948 and then again from 1952 to 1959. In December 1959, Prime Minister John Diefenbaker appointed coach Page Lieutenant-Governor of Alberta. John Percy Page died in Edmonton in 1973.

12

Ethel Catherwood
High jumper

Hometown: Saskatoon

ETHEL CATHERWOOD IS THE ONLY CANADIAN WOMAN TO win an individual gold medal at an Olympic Games track and field meet. She accomplished the feat at Amsterdam in 1928. That year stands out as the first time women were allowed to compete for medals in track and field at the Olympic Games.

Ethel was born in Hannah, North Dakota, in April 1908. Her parents were farmers and they became homesteaders in Saskatchewan when Ethel was an infant. After a few trips back and forth between Hannah and their homestead, the Catherwood family moved to Canada for good in 1910.

Ethel was the best athlete anyone at the Champagne School in Scott, Saskatchewan, had ever seen. At a district track and field meet, her first competition, she set a new school record of 3 feet 10 inches in the high jump. The techniques of the period all used a variation of the scissors jump, which keeps the athlete in an upright and sitting position all the way over the bar. Imagine wearing tied-on, double-bladed skates in the NHL and you'll get an idea of how different Ethel's technique was in comparison to modern standards. The most important thing to remember is that 3 feet 10 inches was a very good jump for a young girl at the public school level in 1922.

In Ethel's 17th year, her family moved off the farm and into town. In Saskatoon, Ethel made a strong impression on the local sport scene where she played softball and basketball and competed in several track and field events for coach Joe Griffith.

In the 1920s, women's rights advocates fought for equality between the sexes. Acceptance was hard for athletes like Ethel at that time. Nothing came easy and the debate raged in the sports world as to the appropriateness of women taking part in vigorous athletic activity. Many critics believed such activity might harm a woman's ability to bear children. Others said flat out that women were simply too frail to take part. Nobody mentioned the heavy farm work that women did every day, after the house was cleaned.

When the International Olympic Committee announced the inclusion of women in the 1928 Olympics, the organizing committees from some countries voiced their objection. Canada's Olympic Committee, particularly one of its prominent members, A.S. Lamb, put our country in that group during the debate on sending women to the Games.

In spite of Lamb's ill-conceived position, Ethel's coach, Joe Griffith, reasoned that other Canadian officials would come around and do the right thing. And they did — Canada decided to send a team to Amsterdam and Ethel Catherwood was determined to be a member of it.

In 1926 at a track and field meet in Regina, Ethel set a world record in the high jump. The press dubbed her the "Saskatoon Lily" — a reference to her long, slender frame and her considerable beauty.

The Prairie public was enamoured with her exploits. Just a few months after her 19th birthday, Ethel made the journey east on the train to assemble with the rest of Canada's 1928 Olympic team for the voyage to Europe. She'd be a member of what the press started calling the "Marvellous Six" — along with runners Fanny Bobbie Rosenfeld, Myrtle Cook, Ethel Smith, Jane Bell and Jean Thompson. The six got to know each other on the Atlantic crossing and began to think and act like a team.

In the high-jump competition, Ethel pulled off her trademark competition move by wearing her bulky sweat suit until the bar reached 5 feet, or until she missed — whichever came first. The move usually freaked her opponents out. At 5 feet, Ethel took off the suit and left both Carolina Gisolf of Holland and the USA's Mildred Wiley in her dust for silver and bronze when she cleared 1.59 metres and claimed her Amsterdam gold medal. The international press was infatuated with Ethel's beauty and a New York reporter called her the most beautiful woman at the Olympics.

The Canadian women made history in Amsterdam. The Marvellous Six became the "Matchless Six" when they won two gold medals, one silver and a bronze and helped Canada to a fourth-place finish — the best ever for our country. As well, the team amassed 34 points to easily outdistance the much larger and better-financed second-place women's team from the USA.

The Matchless Six, sprint champion Percy Williams and the rest of the 1928 team came home to well-deserved praise and celebrations that followed the medallists across the country as they travelled back to their respective hometowns and cities.

Ethel turned down a reported Hollywood movie deal, but left for the U.S., with her sister, immediately after her homecoming. Rumours of a torrid, heartbreaking Olympic love affair between Catherwood and American athlete Harold Osborn circulated at the time and have persisted. Osborn won double gold in the 1924 Paris Olympics, capturing both the high jump and the decathlon. He was married to another woman in the fall of 1928 in Colorado and remained in the marriage until his death in 1975. Eventually Ethel married, becoming Ethel Mitchell, and settled down to domestic life in San Francisco.

Following the Amsterdam Olympics, Lamb spoke out one more time against women competing. The Canadian Olympic Committee ignored his rant and he disappeared from the Canadian Olympic scene.

Ethel Catherwood died in obscurity in 1987.

13

Ada Mackenzie
Golf

⟨⟨⟩⟩

Hometown: Toronto

ADA MACKENZIE WAS BORN IN 1891 IN TORONTO IN THE middle of what was clearly a man's world. As a child, Ada was frustrated trying to find sports activities that were set up for girls. So her competitive hunger was never quite fulfilled.

At Havergal College, a private school for the girls of affluent families, Ada's love of athletics bloomed. She excelled at tennis, basketball, cricket, figure skating and hockey, playing on the school team in each of those sports. Ada won the Havergal Cup three straight times as the college's top athlete. No one since has matched Ada's feat of nearly a century ago.

After graduation in 1911, Ada stayed at the school to become a special sports instructor. She was better than any of her teachers and the school wanted sports for women to advance so they kept her on. Ada was their woman. She believed that girls could benefit greatly from the rigours of athletic competition and passed that belief on to her students. But low pay for teachers, especially for women, frustrated her just as much as male domination in sports.

In 1914 Ada took a job at the Canadian Imperial Bank of Commerce. She felt that the banks might offer more opportunity for a woman with drive. She worked there until 1930. On weekends Ada golfed. Like her mom and dad before her, Ada could find her way around a golf course. In 1919 at the age of 27 she won the Canadian Women's Open. Her career on the course was launched.

Ada would go on and golf well into her seventies. She rounded our her considerable list of golf credits by adding 8 Canadian Women's Senior Titles, 9 Ontario Women's Senior Championships, 10 victories in the Toronto Tournament and 2 trips to the finals of the U.S. Amateur Women's Championship. She played for Scotland by special request at the British Ladies Open in 1929 and was named Canada's Female Athlete of the Year in 1933 by the Canadian Press. All in all, it was a pretty fantastic career, but Ada had much more going on than just golf.

Ada was never happy with the fact that women were treated differently than men in sports, in business or in life. She grew fed up with having restricted tee-times forced on her because of her sex, of being told she couldn't golf on weekends because that was the men's time. She grew tired of being made to feel like a second-class citizen who was supposed to find a man and be content staying home to look after the house while letting the men do all the thinking and have all the fun. Ada didn't see life that way at all. So she changed the rules and dragged the old boys of golf into the twentieth century.

In 1924 Ada went personally from one investor to the next on her own to sell shares in a radical new golf course idea. The very notion of a woman selling shares for her own business was revolutionary. The wealthy women of Toronto flooded her with support.

Ada was adamant that she could raise the money and put together a $30,000 investment fund. In 1924 that was enough money to build a golf course and that's what Mackenzie did. She proudly threw open the doors of the Ladies Golf and Tennis Club of Toronto. The club was, and is, open only to women and girls as members. Men can play as guests but premium times and weekends are reserved for members only. And the members are all women. The Ladies Golf Club of Toronto stands to this day as the only club in North America that caters exclusively to women.

In 1926 Ada indulged another of her passions while also feeding her competitive instinct. She and her ballroom dance partner became Canadian waltz champions. When Ada set her mind on a target in any walk of life she seemed to hit it. She was just that determined.

Ada championed causes for women at all turns. In 1928 her hard-fought battle to establish an Ontario Junior Ladies Championship was won and that event debuted in the province. Ada long reasoned that sports were as good for girls as they were for boys. It saddened her to see all the resources being directed toward the men, so she fought for her convictions and she changed things for the better.

In 1930 Ada raised the investment capital she needed to quit her job at the bank and open her own manufacturing business. Ada Mackenzie Limited specialized in the design and manufacture of a line of clothing made specifically for active women. For the first time, women participating in sports could buy clothing designed for the task.

Ada's company met with great success and she ran it herself for nearly 40 years. Her line of apparel became well known around the world for quality and practicality. She sold her firm upon retirement from the day-to-day business world in 1959.

Ada never retired from golfing though. She finished sixth in her last tournament. Her final bows came in Ottawa at the Canadian Senior Women's Golf Championship in 1969. She was 78.

Ada made a point to get out and swing the clubs for fun until her final summer. She died in January 1972 at the age of 81.

14

Normie Kwong
(Lim Kwong Yew)
Football

⌘

Hometown: Calgary

NORMIE KWONG'S PARENTS IMMIGRATED TO CANADA from Canton Province in China in the early 1920s. To get here, they each had to pay a special $500 head tax to the Government of Canada. The tax was imposed specifically on the Chinese people; it was supposed to help control immigration. It took most of the Kwong family's life savings — $500 was a sizable sum then — but they believed it to be worth every penny.

Being Chinese immigrants, the Kwongs were prohibited from seeking employment in all but the most menial and dangerous jobs. They weren't allowed to vote. They weren't allowed to own property or land. Still, they and thousands of others came to find a better life in Canada. The Kwongs settled in Calgary. Shortly after they arrived in Alberta, the *Chinese Exclusion Act* put a halt to immigration from China altogether. This Act lasted from 1923 until 1947. It remains a stain on the fabric of our nation.

In 1929 the Kwongs joyfully welcomed a new baby into the family. The tiny boy would make a mark in this world

— they just knew it. They named him traditionally, Lim Kwong Yew. On the high school football fields of Calgary he became Normie — Normie Kwong — the "China Clipper."

In 1947 the *Chinese Exclusion Act* was finally struck down and Canadians of Chinese descent were allowed to vote in federal, provincial and municipal elections for the very first time. The Kwong family celebrated their new status.

In 1948 the Kwongs celebrated again. This time they cheered their son Normie's good fortune. The Calgary Stampeders wanted him to play football in the Canadian Football League. The team signed Normie to play fullback. It was a great honour. He was only 18.

In the fall of 1948 the Kwongs celebrated yet again as did the entire Chinese community. So did the city of Calgary and the Province of Alberta and the entire Western Canada. The Stampeders won the Grey Cup and hometown-hero Normie became the youngest player to ever win in the CFL's championship game. He still holds that honour.

Normie became a hero to Chinese kids all across Canada and to everyone who cheered for the underdog. He was the first Chinese-Canadian to become a sports star. He wasn't tall at 5 feet 10 inches, and he wasn't particularly big at 170 pounds. But he was fearless and punishing as a runner, and once he broke into the open field, he could fly. The Calgary fans loved him.

After three seasons with the hometown Stamps, Normie moved north to Edmonton. It was 1951 and Normie was teamed up with another great running back, Johnny Bright, to form one of the most potent backfields in the CFL. Once the Eskimo fans forgave Normie for being born in Calgary, they cheered for him heartily. They cheered even more than that when Bright and Kwong ran the Eskimos straight into the record books.

Edmonton established a dynasty and ran off three straight Grey Cups in the mid-1950s (1954, 1955 and 1956). The China Clipper was a huge reason why. In the last two of those seasons, 1955 and 1956, Normie won the treasured Schenley Award as Canada's Outstanding CFL Player. His 1955 championship season was so impressive that he beat out legendary hockey star Rocket Richard of the Montreal Canadiens for Canada's Athlete of the Year honours, as voted on by the nation's sportswriters. Normie was enormously popular with reporters and fans, from one side of the country to the other.

Normie was always a true gentleman and a great ambassador for football. He left everything he had on the field in every game he played. He was respected both by his teammates and by his opponents. Normie was a role model. That's a precious commodity in any community.

Normie played for the Edmonton Eskimos for the last 10 years of his career. When he retired in 1960 at 31 years of age, his list of football achievements was impressive — in all, he held 30 CFL records. He rushed for over 9000 yards and averaged 5.2 yards per carry. He was an All-Canadian All-Star five times and appeared in the Grey Cup seven times during his 13-year career as a player. He was on the winning side four times. Kwong was selected to the CFL Hall of Fame in 1969 and is a member of Canada's Sports Hall of Fame.

After retirement, Normie focused on new goals. He settled in Calgary with his wife, Mary, and together they built a life away from football, raising four sons. Normie took his responsibilities as a citizen seriously and served as National Chairman to Canada's Council on Multiculturalism; he served as Calgary's Easter Seals Honorary Chairman; and in 1988 became the president and general manager of his old team, the Calgary Stampeders. The China Clipper was back with his first team.

One year later in 1989 as co-owner of the Calgary Flames, Normie won a Stanley Cup ring. That accomplishment makes Normie Kwong the only man to win both the Grey Cup of football and the Stanley Cup of hockey.

In 1998, at the age of 69, Normie Kwong — the China Clipper — was made a Member of the Order of Canada.

15

Fanny Bobbie Rosenfeld
All around

Hometown: Barrie, Ontario

IN 1950 FANNY BOBBIE ROSENFELD WAS SELECTED CANADA'S most outstanding athlete of the half-century — a fitting tribute for our greatest ever all-around athlete.

Fanny was born in Russia in 1903 and came to Canada as an infant when her family immigrated shortly thereafter. The Rosenfelds settled in Barrie, Ontario, and once Fanny reached the school playground it became obvious that she was very gifted athletically. Fanny became Bobbie to her friends and she excelled at softball, basketball, tennis, hockey and almost all the track and field events where she took on and beat all comers — boys and girls. Her dad was her biggest fan. He rarely missed a game or a match if his daughter was taking part. Bobbie grew, secure and loved.

In 1922 the family moved south to Toronto and Bobbie expanded her competitive horizons. Before too long she was a star in the team-sport leagues around the city and was challenging Canadian records in a variety of track and field events. She persuaded her employer, Pattersons Chocolates, to form a track team for the upcoming Ontario Championships: Bobbie constituted the entire team.

In the summer of 1925 she pulled on her Pattersons'

jersey and single-handedly rewrote the record books on the fields at the Ontario Ladies Track and Field Championships in Toronto. In a one-day competition, Bobbie won the 220-yard sprint, the 120-yard hurdles, the long jump, the discus and the shot put. As well, she finished second in the 100-yard sprint and the javelin. Pattersons took the women's team trophy with Bobbie the sole member of the team. Her dad cheered himself hoarse that day.

As the Amsterdam Olympics of 1928 approached, the International Olympic Committee made a decision to allow women to compete for the first time in track and field. It was a contentious move in an era when sport was considered by many to be the sole domain of men. A national championship meet was organized to determine who would represent Canada at those Summer Games. Bobbie set new records in the running long jump, the standing long jump and the discus. She just missed the world mark in the 100-metre race. Rosenfeld would anchor Canada's first-ever Women's Olympic team.

She was a tremendous leader. Bobbie and her new teammates, Myrtle Cook, Ethel Catherwood, Jean Thompson, Jane Bell and Ethel Smith, were eventually dubbed the Matchless Six by the press. They left for Amsterdam filled with great expectations and thoroughly enjoyed their voyage to Europe with the rest of Canada's Olympic team.

In Amsterdam Bobbie had to make some hard decisions. The 100-metre final and the discus had conflicting start times so Rosenfeld withdrew from the field event to focus on the sprint. The drama of the race heightened considerably when teammate Myrtle Cook, a solid pre-race favourite, was disqualified for two false starts. Bobbie was left to carry

Canada's colours with Ethel Smith, while Cook sobbed on the sidelines.

The race was a classic. American champion Betty Robinson broke into an early lead and then, from the midway point, Bobbie closed the gap to finish in a dead heat. The judges were split, with two contending that Robinson had won and two stating that the American had illegally broken the tape with her extended arms and not her body and that Bobbie was the winner. In 1928 there was neither photo nor videotape available to provide the evidence needed to solve the problem. A.S. Lamb, the Canadian team manager, stepped in and told the head judge to award the gold medal to the American. He advised Bobbie that it would be unladylike and un-Canadian to complain. Bobbie settled for silver. Ethel Smith took bronze. Lamb had not wanted the women to compete in the first place.

Bobbie next competed in the 800-metre race. Canadian teammate Jean Thompson was favoured to win but she injured her leg training and struggled during the race. Bobbie decided to let the field and a medal go; she dropped out of contention to run beside Thompson, encouraging her teammate to finish, which they did together. That selfless act of their leader, Bobbie, bonded the team completely.

On the final day of the track meet Bobbie would lead off for Canada's 4 × 100-metre relay team. At stake was the Women's team title. The Canadian women had accumulated as many points as the 18-member team from the USA. Whoever won the relay would win the Olympic crown.

When the gun sounded, Bobbie fired into a lead that the Canadian team never gave up. Myrtle Cook blazed through her run to seal the victory and gain some redemption. The team set a new world record and won Olympic gold, along with the Women's team title. They came home to parades, accolades and adulation — heroes all.

Bobbie retired from amateur sports in 1931. In 1929 a severe attack of arthritis had kept her bedridden for eight months and on crutches for almost a year afterwards. She recovered and went on to win awards in hockey and softball, but her arthritis returned in 1931 and forced her into retirement. Her condition was just too painful for the demands of elite-level training. She played team sports around Toronto for the next few years, establishing herself as a champion for the advancement of women in sport.

In 1937 she turned her attention from the field of play to the world of sports journalism and for the next 20 years wrote a column in the *Globe and Mail*.

Bobbie's writing reflected her love of competition and her high ideals, and she introduced many of Canada's greatest female athletes to her readers. She never stopped fighting for the recognition of women in sports.

Bobbie died in 1969.

16

Miss Supertest
Unlimited class powerboat

⊶⊷

Built in London and Sarnia, Ontario

WHEN WORLD WAR II ENDED, CANADIANS REJOICED. THE armies were disbanded and the warriors came home to build lives and celebrate the freedom they fought for. The economy started to roll; jobs became plentiful; families grew. People took to cottage country in record numbers, clearing sites, building summer homes and buying fast powerboats by the thousands.

The Thompson family of London, Ontario, owned the Supertest Petroleum Company. Anyone over 50 will likely remember the familiar orange-and-black stations. To the Thompsons, power boating became a quest. In 1952 they commissioned Sarnia boat builder Les Stauder to build *Miss Supertest II*. They were anxious to replace and improve the original *Miss Supertest*. They wanted to make some noise out on the growing powerboat-racing circuit.

The new boat was 31 feet long with an aluminum and plywood hull. As an unlimited hydroplane, she was designed to fly. A 2000-horsepower Rolls-Royce Griffin engine powered her 13-inch prop through a British-designed gearbox. At top speed, the only parts actually in the water were half of the prop, half a metre or so of rudder and two grapefruit-sized spots on the lower hull. In 1955 she flew to a new Canadian speed record of 154.854 miles per hour.

In 1956 *Miss Supertest II* was a challenger for the prestigious Harmsworth Trophy. The cup was symbolic of the World Championship. *Miss Supertest II* lost to an American boat. It was the USA's 37th straight win and the Thompsons wanted to break that hold.

In November 1957 on chilly Lake Ontario waters off Picton, Art Astbury piloted *Miss Supertest II* to a new world-speed record of 184.45 miles per hour. The Supertest camp was happy and Canadian power-squadron fans celebrated the amazing feat, but there was a cloud. Earlier in the season the Harmsworth had gone to the USA again. The Thompsons would spend the winter figuring out a way to go even faster.

Over the 1958 season crewmember and mechanic Bob Hayward of Embro, Ontario, was asked to supervise the building of *Miss Supertest III*. She'd be lighter and more powerful than her predecessors and she'd boast a 2000-horsepower Rolls-Royce Griffon engine. In the spring of the year, before the new boat was ready, Bob drove *Miss Supertest II* to the winner's circle at the St. Clair International Trophy regatta in Michigan. But the Harmsworth eluded them yet again. It was time to bring out the new boat to see what she could do.

In 1959 Bob drove *Miss Supertest III* through tests but never opened her all the way to find her top speed. Her total cost was $40,000, but she was 1000 pounds lighter and potentially much faster than the *Miss S-II*. They'd find out soon enough.

In 1959 the Harmsworth was held on the Detroit side

of the Detroit River. Fans lined both banks, but the Windsor side cheered the loudest when Hayward and *Miss Supertest III* won the race for Canada. The 39-year U.S. grip on the World Championship was finally broken. Hayward, the crew and the Thompson family sprayed champagne all over each other.

In 1960 the powerboat world settled in at Lake Ontario near Picton once again. This time Bob Hayward in *Miss Supertest III* defended the Harmsworth Trophy in front of the hometown crowd.

In 1961 the event moved to the Bay of Quinte just off Deseronto, and Bob completed the hat trick, winning the third straight Harmsworth title. *Miss Supertest III* was the fastest boat in the world and she was Canadian.

A month later Bob was in the cockpit of *Miss Supertest II* contesting for the silver cup in the Detroit River. In the first heat, Bob struck a buoy and was disqualified. His strategy for heat two was simple: Get out front and stay out front. If he didn't it would be a short weekend for the Canadian team.

Bob's chance came when a gap opened between the Detroit boat *Miss US-1* and Seattle's *Century 21*. Bob pushed the throttle open and shot through the gap. Then it all came apart and the boat lost control. *Miss Supertest II* rolled, bounced and then rolled again. She was breaking up. Bob was hurled into the river. He went limp.

Bud Saile, who was driving *Thunderbolt*, jumped into the water to rescue the injured Hayward from the overturned boat. Bob was already dead by the time the attending physician reached the crash scene to examine him — his neck was broken. He'd died instantly.

The race was cancelled immediately. Bob Hayward was the first hydroplane driver in 11 years to be killed during a race. The entire community mourned his passing.

After Bob's funeral back in the village of Embro, the Thompson family decided to suspend their racing program for good. *Miss Supertest II* was salvaged from the river but lost in a fire some years later. *Miss Supertest III* remains on display at the Ontario Science Centre in Toronto.

The British International Trophy — the Harmsworth Trophy — rests in a case at the Royal Yacht Club in England, where it was first raced for in 1903.

17

Marilyn Bell
Distance swimmer

Hometown: Toronto

WHEN MARILYN BELL WAS STILL IN SCHOOL, HER PARENTS encouraged her to take up swimming. It was a good way to exercise year-round. So she joined the Lakeshore Swimming Club in Port Credit, just west of Toronto. Marilyn wasn't quite fast enough for the speed events, but her stamina was way above average and her determination was exceptional. She soon became a student of legendary distance-coach Gus Ryder. Gus loved athletes with heart.

By 1953 Marilyn, almost 16 years old, had already established herself as one of the top distance swimmers in the region and a favourite of coach Ryder. She won the Lou Marsh Trophy that year. Early in the summer of 1954, she travelled with her team to New Jersey to take part in the gruelling 26-mile Atlantic City Marathon. Marilyn kept on swimming, while others yielded to pain and fatigue, to become the first woman to ever complete that race. She came home to a champion's welcome.

Later that summer, as a promotion, the Canadian National Exhibition and the *Toronto Telegram* newspaper offered popular American champion Florence Chadwick $10,000 if she could become the first swimmer to ever cross

Lake Ontario. Chadwick had just completed the fastest-ever crossing of the English Channel to worldwide notice and acclaim. The CNE needed to boost flagging attendance in the latter part of the summer and it put up the prize money with the stipulation that the offer was good only to Chadwick. The U.S. swimmer accepted the exclusive offer and that attracted Marilyn's attention.

Marilyn reasoned that the money should be a prize awarded to the first swimmer to make the difficult crossing. But the CNE offer stood and Chadwick alone would get the money if she finished. Marilyn decided to put her Canadian pride on the line and turn it into a race. She was determined to go at least one stroke farther than Chadwick, no matter what happened out in the lake. Slowly but surely, Marilyn grew determined to do what no one else had ever done — to swim all the way across Lake Ontario.

At 11 p.m. on September 9, 1954, just as Florence was entering the cold waters of the lake, Marilyn waded in at Youngstown, New York. She walked out into the water with another great Canadian marathon swimmer: in 1951 Winnie Roach Leuszler of St. Thomas, Ontario, had been the first Canadian to ever swim the English Channel. The women were accompanied by coach Gus Ryder and a news reporter in Marilyn's support boat, which was sponsored by the *Toronto Star*.

Ryder had turned to the *Toronto Star* for sponsorship when the CNE refused to open the prize money up to anyone who could make the crossing. The *Star* and the CNE sponsor, the *Telegram*, were bitter rivals. Much was made in the *Star* of Marilyn's patriotism and decision to swim even though the money was guaranteed exclusively to an

American. So Marilyn was already on the minds of many fans when she waded into the water to swim to her destiny.

The currents were strong and high winds whipped the lake into a mean chop. The swimmers were forced to take a course that lengthened the already extreme 51.5-kilometre (32-mile) crossing. They fought fatigue, floating weeds and overly curious lamprey eels. Florence Chadwick was first to give in to the elements. As she was being pulled over the side of her support boat, the two Canadians, Marilyn and Winnie, swam on into the cooling night.

As if the forces of nature weren't enough to overcome, the swimmers had to cross through polluted waters and an ugly oil spill. Their stomachs churned and their bodies grew numb from the cold. It was all too much for Winnie and she also elected to leave the water. Marilyn's exceptional determination was all that was left to push the teenager home.

At times, Marilyn floated on her back to rest and gather her strength, but whenever that happened she was at the mercy of the currents. Ryder screamed out encouragement to keep her moving toward the distant shore. There were moments when her strength seemed gone, but somewhere she found more, and somehow she kept swimming.

As Marilyn struggled on, the crowd at the CNE grew. Hourly radio reports live from the scene kept the city and the whole country up-to-date on her progress. She was becoming a sensation. Local stations played a song about her. By sunset, 100,000 men, women and children lined the CNE shoreline and when Marilyn made her landing — after 21 numbing hours in the lake — they let out a roar of approval. Marilyn Bell was proclaimed to be the First Lady of the Lake.

In the end, CNE officials and the *Toronto Telegram* managers came to their senses and gave the $10,000 cash prize to Marilyn. The public never would have forgiven them otherwise. The City of Toronto honoured her with a grand parade and she received over $50,000 in cash and gifts from fans all across the country. She told the press that day: "As corny as it sounds . . . , I did it for Canada."

A year later on July 31, 1955, Marilyn became the youngest swimmer to ever cross the English Channel. Then, in 1956 on August 23 she made her second attempt to swim the treacherous Juan de Fuca Strait and became the first woman to ever cross these treacherous waters between Vancouver Island and the mainland.

The Juan de Fuca Strait crossing was Marilyn Bell's last marathon. The First Lady of the Lake retired from distance swimming at 18 years of age, married U.S. swimmer Joe Di Lascio and moved to New Jersey, where they settled down and raised four children.

18

George Knudson
Golf

Hometown: Winnipeg

GEORGE KNUDSON GREW UP IN WINNIPEG DURING WORLD War II. There wasn't a lot of money for extras. If it wasn't food or rent, it was extra. There wasn't much left over for sports equipment.

After the war George began to hang around the nearby St. Charles Golf and Country Club with his buddies. He learned how to find lost golf balls and sell them back to the duffers as seconds — at a greatly reduced rate. He learned how to shag balls and how to caddy. He learned how to measure the course in strides. He learned to feel the wind blow across a fairway.

George learned how to golf too and was the club's junior champion by the time he was 14. The young champ also loved to sneak off with his pals for a cigarette behind the caddy shack. He started to smoke young.

In 1954 George proudly represented St. Charles at the provincial Junior Championship and won the cup for his home clubhouse trophy case. He repeated a year later and then went on to take the Canadian Junior title. He was only 18 and he looked cool with the aviator-style sunglasses. They became a trademark.

In 1959 George qualified for the Professional Golf Association (PGA) tour. In 1961 he won his first title on the big tour at Coral Gables in Florida. Two years later he won the Portland Open. George looked so smooth walking down the fairway — shades, dark sweaters, tall and lean. He always had a smoke hanging out of his mouth. A lot of golfers did back then. Everybody did. It was a time when the cigarette barons were allowed to use models dressed as doctors having a smoke after surgery. Nobody really believed how deadly the habit was yet. That came later.

From his first swings on the tour the golf world was blown away by George's beautiful and effortless swing. He called his style "stillness within motion." When George stood at the tee, everyone, including his opponents, stopped to watch. He had great presence on those PGA tees. His swing is still studied and copied today.

George pioneered conditioning in the game of golf. Common belief held that golfers didn't need to worry about staying in shape, that they'd walk themselves into shape on the golf course. But George disagreed. He worked out a custom program with legendary Canadian fitness guru Lloyd Percival. It was designed specifically to make him stronger and more flexible. He focused on those muscle groups that helped him maintain perfect balance through his perfect swing. As a result, George's long game kept him at the top of his sport through a great golden era.

In 1964 George won the Fresno Open. In 1967 he added the Greater New Orleans Open, and then in 1968 he won both the Phoenix and Tucson Opens. He was the golf king of Arizona.

Most weekends George was in the hunt on Sunday and

the country tuned in on TV to watch him come home. He played with Arnold Palmer, Jack Nicklaus, Gary Player — and in 1969 he took the whole country on a Sunday drive through Georgia in the springtime when he came within a single shot of winning the biggest tournament on the planet, the Masters at Augusta. George Archer won the title and the ceremonial green jacket, but George Knudson won a country. Canadians were glued to the TV watching the venerable proceedings and our George was right in the middle of it. He celebrated by having a smoke.

In 1972 at 35, George won his last big tournaments, the Kaiser International Open and the Robinson Open. In all, George won eight PGA trophies — more than any other Canadian on the tour so far. He also added five CPGA titles to his credit list.

George played the tour into the late 1970s. By the time he retired from the grind of the full-time tour, he'd elevated the popularity of the game in Canada. New courses were being built all over, and existing courses were busier than ever.

In the spring of 1987 George was sharpening his game and planning to join the Senior PGA tour. He would reach the age of eligibility on his 50th birthday in June. He looked forward to getting his card and competing with his old rivals again. There was good money on the senior tour and George's drive was as sweet as it ever had been.

Just days before his birthday, George suffered severe chest pains after his regular workout. Fearing a heart attack, he went to the nearest hospital. It was worse than he'd imagined. George's chest X-rays revealed lung cancer in an advanced stage.

George's experience with chemotherapy left him weakened. He did gather enough strength to play at a Legends Tournament in Austin, Texas. The crowd, as always, applauded the legendary swing. The day was filled with emotion for George and for his family. It was his last public appearance. He flew to another tournament on Rhode Island, but he was too weak to play and had to return home.

George died in Toronto in 1989 at the age of 51. His best days were still ahead.

19

Russ Jackson
Football

Hometown: Hamilton

RUSS JACKSON WAS THE BEST ATHLETE AT WESTDALE Collegiate in Hamilton. In fact, he was one of the best high school athletes in the country back in the early 1950s. Russ starred at basketball and hockey, but his true strength was as the quarterback of the Westdale football team — he was the best ever produced in Canada in that position.

Jackson graduated high school and became an all-star at McMaster University in two sports, basketball and football. While with his team, the Marauders, his exploits on the football field drew the attention of the Ottawa Rough Riders — now the Renegades — of the Canadian Football League. They signed him in 1958. Coach Frank Clair liked the Canadian quarterback's quiet confidence.

Russ raised some eyebrows around the league when he negotiated his own deal. He asked for, and received, a $500 signing bonus plus an open ticket from Ottawa to Toronto. He intended to keep up his studies and earn his teacher's certificate. In Russ's mind, sports and education were equally important. As well, he knew that football wouldn't last forever. Not like an education.

In Ottawa Russ became a platoon quarterback with Ron

Lancaster, an import from the U.S. college ranks. Neither of the future Hall of Fame stars was happy with the situation. The competition between them was intense. It was magnified by the contrast in their styles. Lancaster was a gung-ho leader, coal-mining-country tough and outspoken. Jackson was more reserved, more soft-spoken and less opinionated. The rivalry extended off the field. Jackson and Lancaster were respectful teammates but they were never pals.

Coach Clair and the Ottawa Rough Rider management and loyal fans were thrilled in 1960 when the young quarterbacks fought so hard to win the starter's role that they took the Rough Riders to the Grey Cup. The nation's capital fans looked forward to years of bickering between the two quarterbacks. But there was only room for one rollout passer in Ottawa.

When Lancaster was traded to Saskatchewan, Russ stepped into the Riders starting quarterback spot and never gave it up again. By 1962 Russ won his first of six selections as a CFL all-star. In 1963 he led the league in passing and was named the CFL's Outstanding Player of the Year. While he was ringing up the records, Russ was also wrapping up his studies and becoming a high school teacher. Eventually, Jackson upgraded his education enough to become a principal.

Russ had to fight back stereotypes to achieve greatness as a quarterback. General managers, coaches and assistant coaches who come up through the U.S. college system dominate CFL management. Because they often handle the scouting duties, they naturally tend to look south, to familiar territory to find their stars. Their faith in Canadian homegrown quarterbacks has always been shaky. That's what makes Russ's assault on the record books even more exciting — knowing that he had to fight such enormous odds just to get the chance to show what he could do.

In 1966 Russ took the Grey Cup back to Ottawa. His all-star season culminated in another Schenley Player of the Year Award and he sat at the top of most quarterback statistic categories. In the Grey Cup game in Vancouver he was up against his old rival Ron Lancaster. "The Little General" Lancaster beat Russ's team 29–14. Jackson, as the leader of the Rough Riders, stepped forward to take the heat for the loss. He gained a lot of admiration that day.

Two years later Russ had his team back in the final. In a great game in Toronto he out-threw a talented passer, Peter Liske of the Calgary Stampeders, to win the Grey Cup 24–21 for the Riders. Russ's critics grew silent and Ottawa grew noisy in celebration.

In 1969 Russ Jackson pieced together the perfect season. With his mind set on the Grey Cup in Montreal in November Russ rallied his team for a championship push. He was selected as the CFL's outstanding player for the third time and was named to his sixth all-star team. The Saskatchewan Roughriders won the west, so the final was a football dream: Russ Jackson against his archrival Ron Lancaster for one final time.

In his last and most memorable Grey Cup appearance, Russ approached perfection. He threw, for a record, four touchdown passes and led Ottawa to its third Grey Cup of the 1960s. The score was 29–11. It wasn't even close. Russ was clearly the quarterback of the era.

Russ and the team received the Grey Cup on the field from Prime Minister Pierre Trudeau. The PM was a great sports fan. At that moment Russ decided to call it a career.

It couldn't get much better. So he retired right then, at the very highest moment of his career. Russ drove home in his brand-new car — awarded to the Grey Cup's Most Valuable Player, a football legend.

Russ settled in to become an inspirational high school principal who passed on the lessons of a champion to his students. He also served as a frustrated coach in the CFL and is still involved in CFL radio broadcasts. He is without question the greatest Canadian quarterback in the history of football.

20

Northern Dancer
Thoroughbred horse racing

———

Hometown: Oshawa, Ontario

NORTHERN DANCER WAS FOALED ON MAY 27, 1961, LONG after most of the other class of '61 foals were born. He was sired by Windfields Farm's new stallion, Neartic, and was out of Native Dancer mare, Natalma. The little guy had a crooked blaze and three white stockings so he stood out from the start. Northern Dancer, dubbed "The Dancer," was the smallest of the bunch in size, but no one could tell yet that his heart was bigger than all the rest.

When no one bought him for the $25,000 asking price at the yearling sale, his stable owner, E.P. Taylor, decided to keep the little horse. Northern Dancer was trailered over to Fort Erie, Ontario, to work with Taylor's second-string trainer, T.P. Fleming. Since expectations were low, everyone was patient. The idea was just to wait and see what the future might bring.

Northern Dancer was spirited and powerful, with a strong personality, and he loved to run. It's as though he was always trying to prove that size didn't matter. He debuted in early August of 1963, a two year old, and won his first race by over six lengths. He added a second-place finish before winning the Summer Stakes.

The Windfields staff was suitably impressed. Northern Dancer finished his two-year-old season at Woodbine Race Track in Toronto. He won seven times and was second twice in a total of nine starts that year. He also won the respect and love of Horatio Luro, Mr. Taylor's Hall of Fame trainer. His tremendous rookie season earned Northern Dancer the title of Canada's Champion 2-year Old Colt. Pretty good for a little horse nobody wanted.

For a Thoroughbred racehorse, the third birthday is a big one. That's the year the most prestigious and coveted series in all the racing world is within reach — the Triple Crown. The trio of races starts with the Kentucky Derby, and then comes the Preakness and finally, the Belmont Stakes. One victory guarantees the owner big profits. A sweep is a free pass to the realm of equine mythology.

As the 1964 Kentucky Derby approached, the favourite was a big bay from California named Hill Rise. Both he and Northern Dancer were used to the same jockey, Bill Shoemaker, who rode at Woodbine all summer and Santa Anita, California, all winter. Bill had to make a choice for the Derby and he chose Hill Rise, who towered over Northern Dancer at the start. It was May 2nd and the Canadian horse's third birthday was still weeks away, but he was in against the best horses in his age group in North America. With Bill Hartack aboard, Northern Dancer more than stood his ground.

Northern Dancer broke off the final turn at historic Churchill Downs in the lead. He increased his margin to two lengths before Hill Rise made his move. The California horse nearly closed the gap, but Northern Dancer just would not quit. He won the Kentucky Derby in 2:00 minutes flat and wore the rose blanket into the winner's circle at the fabled track. E.P. Taylor, Horatio Luro and the entire country went wild. A Canadian two year old was the horse of the moment.

Two weeks later at the Preakness on Pimlico Race Track in Baltimore, Maryland, Hill Rise was favoured again. And yet again Northern Dancer ignored the odds-makers to win the race. This time his margin of victory was nearly three lengths over Scoundrel, with Hill Rise falling to third. Now Northern Dancer held two jewels of the Triple Crown. He was flirting with the status of racing legend.

After finally getting his third birthday behind him, Northern Dancer travelled north from Maryland to New York's Aqueduct Race Track for the running of the Belmont Stakes. The hectic pace finally caught up with him and a third-place finish ended the Windfields team's dream of winning the Triple Crown.

Northern Dancer came home to Woodbine to easily win the Queen's Plate on June 20 and was named North America's 3-year Old of the Year for his effort. The win at home would be the final victory for the horse Canada had learned to love.

Northern Dancer came down with a bowed tendon soon after his last win. The Windfields vet declared his days as a racer over. He was shipped home to Oshawa's green fields to stand stud for a $10,000 fee — his services guaranteed. It was the bargain of the century. Northern Dancer's first crop of foals produced 2-year Old Colt of the Year, Vice Regal. His second produced Nijinsky, who was undefeated as a two year old. Northern Dancer's offspring were winning at an incredible rate.

In December 1968 Northern Dancer moved to E.P. Taylor's new farm in Maryland, where his services as a stud were booked constantly. His fee climbed steadily through the seventies and by 1980 he commanded $1 million to stand stud. In 1983 at the Keeneland select sale, Sheikh Maktoum of Dubai purchased the colt Snaafi Dancer (by My Bupers and Northern Dancer) for the record-smashing price of $10.2 million in one of the most exciting Thoroughbred auctions ever. That line of the Northern Dancer family tree is credited with reviving the bloodlines of European Thoroughbred racing. Northern Dancer was without peer — the most-prized stallion in the history of the sport of kings.

Northern Dancer retired in 1986 at the age of 25. He died in the fall of 1990 at Windfields Farm in Maryland surrounded by loving stable hands. His body came home to Windfields' Oshawa farm, where he was buried.

21

Harry Jerome
Sprinter

Hometown: Vancouver

HARRY WINSTON JEROME STOOD BY HIS LIFE MOTTO: NEVER give up. He fought through adversity and bias at every turn to become one of the greatest sprinters the sports world has ever known.

Harry was born in Prince Albert, Saskatchewan, but moved to Vancouver when he was 12 years old. Five years later the track coach at North Vancouver High recognized Jerome's natural talent and began to groom him for greater things.

Harry didn't disappoint. He landed a scholarship at the University of Oregon to run for that school's fabled track team. The records began to fall before him. In 1959 at the Olympic Trials in Saskatoon he broke Percy Williams 31-year-old record by clocking the 100-metre sprint in 10 seconds flat. He was the first Canadian to officially hold the world record and his time stood until the Olympics in 1968. Harry held the world record and he was only 18!

As the 1960 Rome Olympic Games approached, the pressure mounted on young Harry. His great promise fuelled hopes of big results and the entire country was expecting Jerome to bring back Canada's first Olympic sprint medal in more than 30 years. But Harry pulled a muscle in the semifinal heat and his quest for gold died right there on the track at Rome's Olympic Stadium. Some sportswriters questioned his heart. None consulted team doctors.

He came home dejected but determined. He overcame his muscle pull and later that year he ran the uniquely North American 100-yard sprint in 9.1 seconds, tying the record of U.S. sprint legend Bob Hayes. Hayes went on to become a star in NFL with the Dallas Cowboys. Harry, on the other hand, buried his head in the books at school and continued collecting credits that eventually earned him a master's degree. Harry was big on education.

In the fall of 1962 more than 1000 athletes and officials travelled to Perth, Australia, for the Commonwealth Games. Among that number were some of the world's fastest sprinters. Harry was favoured to win gold in the 100-metre final, but during the race he crumpled and fell to the track in obvious pain, a ruptured muscle in his left thigh torn terribly. A cast was fashioned to render Harry's leg immobile and he lay alone in the hospital while too many sportswriters declared his career over. None consulted Harry about his imminent demise. If any had, maybe they'd have gained some insight into Harry's heart. Never give up.

Harry fought back. He fought against medical predictions that said he'd never run again. He fought back against a press that called him a quitter. And he fought back against his own inner demons. Harry never quit.

In 1964 Harry Jerome helped the Oregon 4 x 100-relay team set a world record of 38 seconds over the distance. Then he rolled to another Canadian championship and held that title seven times over the course of his career. He then left for the Olympic Games in Tokyo where he won a bronze medal, Canada's first since 1928 when Percy Williams won gold. Harry turned a lot of Canadian fans around in Tokyo.

Two years later in 1966 he completed his impossible comeback by blazing to a new 100-yard sprint record in 9.1 seconds. Later that year at the Commonwealth Games in Kingston, Jamaica, Harry beat a stellar field to capture gold for Canada. He reached his apex that day in the bright Caribbean sun and then went on to win gold in 1967 at the Pan Am Games.

The 1968 Olympics in Mexico City provided Harry's final big moment on the international stage. He moved through the heats and into the final. In the big race he finished just two-tenths of a second behind the winner. Jim Hines of the USA won gold and set a new 100-metre record at 9.9 seconds. The mark he broke was, of course, Harry's — the 10 seconds flat he ran nine years earlier in Saskatchewan. Harry's Commonwealth Games rival, Lennox Miller of Jamaica, won the silver medal, and Charlie Greene of the USA won bronze.

Harry retired at 29 after winning his seventh Canadian title, a gold in the 100-metre at the Pan Am Games in 1969 and spending 10 years at the top of the track world. The injuries took their toll and Harry's speed was diminishing. He had to find new challenges.

Harry taught for a few years and then became a special consultant for Sport Canada, where he worked with children in athletics. He thrived in the job. He was invested as an Officer of the Order of Canada in 1971.

Harry Jerome died suddenly in 1982 of a brain seizure, at just 42. A statue at the University of Saskatchewan, not far from the spot where he set his 100-metre record in 1959, marks his achievements. Each year awards in his name are given to outstanding black Canadian athletes. The Harry Jerome Classic, an international track meet, is held annually in Vancouver.

22

Fergie Jenkins
Baseball

Hometown: Chatham, Ontario

IN THE MIDDLE OF THE 1967 SUMMER AT MAJOR LEAGUE
Baseball's All-Star Game in Anaheim Stadium a lean
sophomore pitcher from Canada took the mound for the
National League team. In the only two innings he pitched,
the young right-hander consecutively struck out six of the
most feared batters in the American League. Among them
were Harmon Killebrew, who'd lead the majors in home
runs that year, Rod Carew, on his way to rookie-of-the-year
honours, and the legendary Mickey Mantle of the New York
Yankees. The six-strikeout performance put the pitcher's name
into baseball's record books. That name is Fergie Jenkins.

Ferguson Arthur Jenkins' ancestors came to Southwestern
Ontario on the Underground Railroad during the U.S. Civil
War. The refugees wanted to live as free and equal citizens
in a country where slavery was illegal. So they settled down
and farmed near Blenheim, just outside of Chatham. Their
family took roots and their babies were born.

Ferguson Arthur Jenkins was born on December 13, 1943.
In the summer his dad travelled south as a young man to play
baseball in America's Negro Leagues. Mr. Jenkins also played
in the Senior Intercounty League when Fergie was a boy.

The father encouraged the son and taught him the fundamentals. He knew that sports could enrich his boy's life. Fergie was already blooming as an athlete — he was a natural — playing baseball, basketball and football at the all-star level, but his first love was hockey and he reached the junior leagues.

Fate stepped in, however, when his baseball team didn't have any pitchers left and Fergie, an outfielder, took the mound for the first time. He found his calling right there that day.

The Philadelphia Phillies spent some time scouting in Ontario and signed the unknown Canadian in 1962. Management decided to turn Jenkins into a relief pitcher. Fergie was happy just to be there. Partway through the 1965 season he was called up to the majors, where he stuck. But for some reason the Phillies couldn't see the young pitcher's talent and Jenkins was dealt in the middle of the following season to the Chicago Cubs, where he became an all-star and went on to win 284 games in the majors. It was the greatest trade the Cubbies ever made.

Cub manager Leo Durocher saw the talent instantly and converted Fergie from a reliever to a starter. The tough old manager loved the 6-foot-5-inch Jenkins' smooth, efficient delivery and his exceptional control. Durocher knew that with time Fergie would become overpowering and develop into a star, maybe even a Hall-o-Famer. Fergie did just that in the middle of one of baseball's most fertile eras for pitchers. Fergie faced legends of the mound like Bob Gibson, Don Drysdale, Juan Marichal and Tom Seaver on a regular basis. He more than held his own.

In Fergie's sophomore summer of 1967 he won 20 games

for a mediocre Cubs club and then registered from 1968 till 1972 with 20, 21, 22, 24 and 20 consecutive wins. Ferguson Jenkins was a strike-throwing machine and he was selected the Sporting News Player of the Year in 1968.

In 1971 in addition to the 24 wins, Fergie did something no Canadian had ever done before and won the Cy Young Award. He was the best pitcher in the National League and he played for the lowly Cubs. A radio commentator of the day described Fergie's biggest pitching liability as being his fellow Cub teammates.

In 1973 Fergie struggled with injuries for the first time in his career and won just 14 games. The next season the Chicago Cubs showed why it's no fluke that they haven't appeared in the World Series since 1945 and traded Fergie to Texas, another mediocre team. Fergie responded by running up 25 wins for the Rangers — the most in his career — and being named Major League Comeback Player of the Year.

In 1976 Fergie went to the Red Sox who were not a contending team. He never did fit in at Boston, and the Sox dealt him back to Texas two years later. He always fit in with the Rangers. Fergie provided an anchor for the unpredictable Rangers and the veteran starter proceeded to win 51 games in four seasons at Arlington.

In 1980 Fergie reached the low point of his career when he was busted with a small amount of cocaine at Exhibition Stadium in Toronto while his team was playing the Blue Jays. A provincial judge waived the guilty verdict and Fergie was never sentenced because of his years of "exemplary conduct." However, Major League Baseball suspended him that September; but things got messy and the ruling was overturned when the players' union stepped in on Fergie's behalf. The whole affair dragged Fergie down. The game he loved so much became more difficult for the great veteran pitcher.

Fergie finished his career back with the Cubs wearing the familiar jersey number 31 for his last two seasons. He retired in 1983 at 39 years of age. Fergie's lifetime earned run average was 3.34. He won 284 games and is the only pitcher to ever record 3000 or more strikeouts while walking fewer than 1000 batters. He had 7 seasons with 20 or more wins and 49 career shutouts.

Fergie was inducted into the Baseball Hall of Fame at Cooperstown, New York, in 1993. In his speech that day he thanked his mother, his father and the country of his birth, Canada.

23

Jocelyn Lovell
Cycling

Hometown: Mississauga, Ontario

JOCELYN LOVELL WAS BORN IN 1950 IN NORWICH, ENGLAND — a city with plenty of bicycles. When the Lovells immigrated to Ontario, they found a society dominated by cars. Bikes were strictly second class and the relationship between drivers and riders was tenuous at best. But traffic be damned, Jocelyn loved cycling. So he pumped his way around the roads west of Toronto, growing stronger day by day.

At 16, Jocelyn went to the Canadian Cycling Championships and won both the Junior and the Senior 1-kilometre time-trial races. The next year he represented Canada at the 1967 Pan Am Games and finished fourth in the 1-kilometre time trial. His results were a wake-up call for Canadian cycling.

In Mexico City in 1968 Jocelyn wore Canada's Olympic team uniform for the first time. He placed sixth in the 1-kilometre time trial. At long last, Canada had a world-class cyclist to lead the pack. Jocelyn didn't disappoint anyone, except himself.

Jocelyn spent 1969 and 1970 consolidating his position as the dominant rider in Canada. In 1969 he defended his senior 1-kilometre time-trial title and added a victory in the 4-kilometre pursuit. A year later he took three titles: in the sprint, the 10-mile races and the 1-kilometre time trial. Jocelyn was winning everything in sight. But it wasn't enough. The cyclist pushed even harder and was fast gaining a reputation for emotional volatility. While some criticized his hotheaded nature, others recognized it as part of the fire that drove him on to greater things.

In 1970 Jocelyn travelled to Edinburgh, Scotland, for the British Commonwealth Games. He captured gold in the 10-mile race, silver in the tandem sprint and bronze in the 1-kilometre time trial, Canada's first big-meet medals since Robert McLeod in 1934. Jocelyn Lovell ended the long drought.

After the 1971 Pan Am Games, Jocelyn appeared to be on form to move up to a higher international level. At that competition he set a meet record in the 1-kilometre time trial that stood for 28 years. At the Canadian Championships he won four separate races in four different events that year.

At the Munich Olympics in 1972, however, Jocelyn became lost amid the also-rans and then swept up in the emotion of the hostage incident that changed the Olympics forever: 11 Israeli hostages, 5 Palestinian extremists and a German policeman died after Palestinians stormed the Israeli dormitory in the Olympic athletes' village. Canada's team was living beside Israel's.

Jocelyn continued his domination of the Canadian championship over the next four years as the Montreal Games of 1976 approached. In 1975 he easily defended his Pan Am Games 1-kilometre time-trial championship. His goal was to make it to his sport's highest level in front of Canadian fans at home in Montreal at the 1976 Olympics. But the breakthrough didn't come.

Jocelyn came away from Montreal with nothing to show but experience. Like many Canadian athletes on the Olympic team, he learned that pressure had to be handled. Many members of Canada's Olympic team failed to do that in Montreal.

Jocelyn's most productive year came in 1978 when he finally broke onto the podium at the World Championships. His second-place finish in his specialty event — the 1-kilometre time trial — put the crown on his 9-year career representing Canada at the Worlds. In Edmonton at the Commonwealth Games he wrote himself into history with three gold medals, to become the event's most-decorated cyclist of all time.

With his strong ranking in the world, his reputation as a fierce competitor fairly won, and his determination honed to a razor edge, Jocelyn was posed to satisfy his Olympic hunger in Moscow in 1980. But his dream, as with the entire Canadian team, was snuffed out after Canada's government decided to join the American-led Olympic boycott protesting the Soviet Union's 1979 invasion of Afghanistan. He was a loud critic of the boycott, but it did no good. And the war in Afghanistan dragged on. Lovell sensed that, at 30, his Olympic quest was drawing to an unfulfilled end.

Jocelyn trained hard through 1981 and 1982 and was again the national champion in the 1-kilometre sprint. He went to Brisbane, Australia, for the Commonwealth Games in his final rip abroad with the national team. It was fitting because he is such a legend in the history of the Commonwealth Games.

After the Brisbane trip, Lovell kept up his conditioning program. While road training alone on Britannia Road just west of Mississauga, Jocelyn was run down from behind by a dump truck. The cyclist who'd won 36 Canadian titles in his glorious career lay crushed and broken in the ditch at the side of the road. His bike was a pile of twisted ruin. His spinal cord was snapped.

Jocelyn survived with intensive emergency care, but he woke up to a devastating reality. He was completely paralyzed from the neck down — a quadriplegic. Jocelyn has been fighting for survival each and every day since.

Jocelyn's athletic achievements helped revive the sport of cycling in Canada. He is the Canadian co-ordinator of cure and research for the Spinal Cord Society.

24

Gary Beck
Top Fuel drag racing

⸫

Hometown: Edmonton

GARY BECK WAS BORN IN SEATTLE, WASHINGTON. AS A teenager, he learned how to drive hot rods and settled in at the local drag strip driving mostly stock, A- and B-class dragsters. He held his own most weekends.

Gary headed north to Edmonton after meeting his future wife, Penny, and followed her home. They were married in 1969. Gary promised to get a job, settle down and forget all about fast cars. He did his best, but the pull was too strong and a year later Gary joined the Capitol City Hot Rod Club.

Hanging out at the garage and coaxing a little more power out of an engine just felt good to Gary. He promised Penny he wouldn't drive but just be part of the team. She knew even then that sooner or later Gary would have to slip behind the wheel.

When Gary took on partner Ken McLean and bought a Top Fuel dragster, he kept his promise and let his friend drive. The team was mired in mediocrity and one thing Gary hated even more than not being able to drive was losing.

In 1972 Gary bought out McLean, made a better sponsor-ship deal and decided that nobody could drive the racer —

called "The Joker" — any faster than he could. He got his Top Fuel licence, trailered the dragster down to his old Seattle neighbourhood, and was blown out of the first Top Fuel race he entered in the very first heat. Gary could plainly see that there was plenty of room for improvement.

The next race on the schedule was the US NHRA Nationals in Indianapolis. So Gary towed the Beck & Lawrence dragster over the Rocky Mountains, across the wide Prairies and into the heartland.

He qualified 10th out of 32 cars. Not bad for his second race — he'd obviously made some adjustments. Then Gary worked patiently through the eliminations and came up against Jerry Ruth, "The King of the Northwest," in the final. Ruth had just set a new National Record at 6.11 seconds in 229 mph on the fast Indy quarter-mile track.

When the Christmas tree lights came down for the final, Beck blew out of the hole fast and the King blew out his engine in the big race. Gary cruised through the quarter-mile to the national title. Two races and he was the champion.

In 1973 he went out and did it all over again by running 5.96 and beating "Cool" Carl Olson in the final. Gary switched his team around that year and attracted so much attention in the Beck & Peets Reliable Engine Service dragster that he became known as the "Quiet Canadian." He didn't say much; he just won all the time.

In 1974 Gary won 59 race titles in 74 runs and captured the National Hot Rod Association Top Fuel World Championships. To do that, he had to beat some of the greatest drivers drag racing has ever known. He shut down big stars like "Big Daddy" Ed Garlits, Shirley "Cha Cha" Muldowney and Don "The Snake" Prudhomme. Gary was lining up with the legends of the sport and leaving them at the line.

In 1975 the winning ways continued for the Quiet Canadian. Gary finished right behind Garlits for the NHRA title. In September at the Super Nationals in Ontario, California, Gary became the first Top Fuel racer to burn through the finish line in the 5.6s when he clocked 5.69 seconds.

Gary went on in his career to continue that pattern and become the first driver to break into the 5.5s, which he did in 1981; the 5.4s, which came in 1982; and the 5.3s, which he hit in 1983. Gary broke through every barrier in front of him and pushed the nitro burners in the Top Fuel class to the limits of their sport.

In the early 1980s, Gary became one of the most dependable drivers on the strip. He finished second in 1980 and 1981 for the NHRA crown and in 1982 was one of the top money earners on the tour. The Beck team was money in the bank.

Gary's best season was in 1983. The Minor and Beck dark blue dragster won four major elimination events and set the lowest times in 10 out of the 12 races they entered. At Florida's famed Gatornationals in the spring they ran a 5.44 to set a new National record. Then in the fall in Fremont, California, at the Golden Gate Nationals Beck blazed to 5.391 — a time he repeated at the World Finals event at Orange County International Raceway before the season ended. When the numbers were added up that year, Gary had 17 out of the fastest 18 runs in Top Fuel history to his credit. To honour the occasion he was named the Winston Champion once again.

Gary retired in 1986 after the World Finals in Pomona, California. He settled down in the southern sunshine in Laguna Nigel, California. Gary ranks in the top six all-time Top Fuel winners in NHRA history. He still loves the smell of burning rubber and the sound of unbridled horsepower that roars from a Top Fuel dragster.

25

Sylvie Bernier
Diving

Hometown: Ste-Foy, Quebec

IN 1956 AT AUSTRALIA'S FIRST OLYMPIC GAMES IN Melbourne, Irene MacDonald won a bronze medal for Canada on the diving 3-metre springboard. It was our first medal ever in the event and it took nearly 30 years for another Canadian to reach the Olympic podium in that discipline. But in 1984 Sylvie Bernier made the wait bearable when she pulled off the big Olympic upset and won a gold medal.

Sylvie started diving in Ste-Foy as a child. Her first attempts off the springboard came when she was just eight years old at the local pool. Sylvie never let her asthma hold her back and threw herself into the sport. She loved the short burst of flight and freedom that came at the end of the board.

By 1973 Sylvie was competing in meets all around the northeast and holding her own against athletes from the big American teams. In 1975, her learning curve swept upward even further when she became a student of Jean Plamondon in Montreal. From there she ventured out onto the world diving stage to make her mark.

By 1980 Sylvie was national champion. But her trip to

the Olympics was scratched when Canada boycotted the Moscow Olympics to protest the Soviet invasion of Afghanistan in 1979. She'd make up for it four years later in Los Angeles.

Sylvie held the Canadian title for five straight years and set the meet record at 544 points. In 1981 her win at Dive Canada was followed up by a second-place finish at the vaunted USA Hall of Fame International meet against the best competition North America could offer. Then Sylvie crossed the Atlantic and placed second at the Bolzano Invitational International in Italy against Europe's best. Sylvie Bernier, asthma and all, was quietly climbing to the top of her sport.

In 1982 Sylvie added a first-place finish at the Can-Am-Mex meet in Torneo, Mexico, while repeating her second-place performances of the previous year in Bolzano and at the Hall of Fame International. Then Sylvie went to the Commonwealth Games in Brisbane to compete for Canada. She was carrying great expectations for a championship but wound up in second behind Jenny Donnet, who was pumped by her home crowd in Australia. The silver medal did not satisfy Sylvie.

In 1982 Sylvie switched coaches and began working with Donald Dion. Sylvie soon became a fixture on leaderboards around the diving world. She took third place in the Pan Am Games, the World University Games and a FINA World Cup event. She won both the USA Hall of Fame International and the Rostock Invitational in East Germany against top-ranked international divers.

In the run-up to the Los Angeles Olympics in 1984, Sylvie prepared by winning at Dive Canada and defending her USA Hall of Fame International title. Still, she was not favoured to win an Olympic medal. The favourites were the strong divers from the host USA team and the rapidly emerging Chinese athletes.

While practising before the event, Sylvie and coach Dion worked relentlessly on Bernier's entries. They felt that improved technique in that crucial area might pull Sylvie up into contention. She focused her attention on the essential elements of her dives and she shut out the rest of the world.

In the qualification round, Sylvie listened to "Flashdance" on her Walkman constantly, taking it off only to dive. She listened to music and ignored everything around her — even the standings and the scores. All that mattered was her next dive. In her mind she replayed the upcoming performance over and over. Each time through she did everything perfectly. She memorized every frame and then nailed the entry on her reverse with pike dive in the third round of the finals to take the lead. She put on her Walkman, pre-played her next dive and never let that lead go.

Sylvie's point total was 530.70 points. That day in Los Angeles it was enough to win gold. Sylvie beat back the charge of USA divers and long-time rivals Kelly McCormick and Chris Seufert, who took silver and bronze respectively. The Chinese divers never got untracked in the competition.

Sylvie took off her Walkman at last. On the podium at the medal ceremony in front of millions of viewers listening to "O Canada" and watching our flag mixed with her smile, Sylvie Bernier became a star and a hero to a new generation of Canadian divers.

One of them was Annie Pelletier. Twelve years later, Annie won bronze on the 3-metre springboard in Atlanta. Sylvie Bernier was her hero.

Sylvie retired after Los Angeles to become a wife, a mother and a television commentator and spokesperson for asthma. She and her husband, Gilles Cloutier, have three daughters.

26

Debbie Brill
High jump

Hometown: Burnaby, B.C.

THE SOUTH OTTER ELEMENTARY SCHOOL IN ALDERGROVE, British Columbia, was so small that team sports were impossible — there just weren't enough students. So the emphasis was on the individual, and the Aldergrove track and field team became a formidable force. In the early sixties, Debbie Brill was the team star and the best high jumper anyone in the region had ever seen.

At 12 years old, Debbie moved up to the Langley Club and set an age-group high-jump mark of 1.32 metres. She started to modify her style and began to use what became known as the "Brill Bend." It quickly became the standard technique for jumpers around the world. By the age of 14, Brill bent her way over the bar at 1.63 metres – an impressive improvement in just two years and a taste of what was to come.

In 1970, at 17 years of age, Debbie became the first North American woman in history to clear 6 feet. Her free-spirited attitude caught the attention of track fans everywhere. Then she won a gold medal at the British Commonwealth Games in Edinburgh, Scotland, with a jump of 1.78 metres. The next year at the 1971 Pan Am Games in Cali, Colombia,

Debbie jumped 1.85 metres (6 feet 3/4 inches) to capture victory. At 17, Debbie was the best high jumper in North America and in the entire British Empire.

In 1972, still just 19 years old, Debbie became a member of Canada's Olympic team and she left for Munich. She qualified for the final and placed eighth after clearing 1.82 metres. Gold went to 16-year-old West German Ulrike Meyfarth, who equalled the world record using the Brill Bend.

In Munich the first terrorist attack of the modern era saw Palestinian extremists murder 11 Israeli Olympic team members in a hostage incident that began at the Olympic village near the Canadian team's quarters. Five of the militants, along with a German policeman, also died. Many of the athletes who were there left Munich with little hope for the survival of the spirit of the Olympic Games. Debbie Brill stopped jumping for two years. She travelled the world. She lived on a houseboat. She came to terms with her competitive spirit.

Debbie started to train seriously again in 1975. By the season's end she was ranked sixth in the world. Brill was back. The 1976 Summer Olympic Games were approaching. Debbie would jump in Montreal wearing Canada's colours. She moved up to fourth in the world rankings prior to the Olympics and put in a huge jump of 1.89 metres going into the Games. She seemed poised to shine. But the pressure was mounting day by day. The expectations of the nation were enormous.

In a misguided attempt to motivate Debbie, a team coach suggested that she'd win the event with a jump of 1.95 metres. The coach reasoned that the statement would motivate the athlete. It didn't. With the stadium packed and millions of her countrymen watching on TV, including the kids from the Aldergrove public school, Debbie became lost in the moment. She didn't even clear 1.75 metres. Debbie wouldn't qualify for the final. She was crushed.

Most critics wrote her off after Montreal. They called her a flake and a choke artist. But she gave them back their empty words. For the second time in her life she had to reinvent herself, and Debbie went to work it out all by herself. Then she came back one more time.

In 1978, in front of an appreciative crowd in Edmonton, Debbie won a silver medal at the Commonwealth Games. In 1979, Debbie went to San Juan, Puerto Rico, and captured bronze for Canada at the Pan Am Games. Then in Montreal, in front of the same crowd she'd disappointed so much in 1976, Debbie won the World Cup with a leap of 1.96 metres (6 feet 5 inches). She was the best jumper in the world as the season closed. The critics had all but disappeared.

Debbie's third Olympics should have been in Moscow. She'll never know how high the bar would have climbed because Canada's Olympic team joined the USA in a boycott of the Moscow Games of 1980. The Americans led the boycott to protest the Soviet Union's invasion of Afghanistan in 1979. The Soviet Army stayed on in Afghanistan for another nine years after the Olympic closing ceremonies. The boycott had no effect whatsoever except to leave the athletes who didn't go there with an empty place inside.

Debbie kept on high jumping after Moscow. In 1982, just months after the birth of her son, she set a world indoor record at 1.99 metres. It was her best-ever jump in competition. Later that season, in Brisbane, Australia, she won her last big meet at the Commonwealth Games, where she captured gold.

At Los Angeles in 1984 Debbie placed fifth to close out her Olympic career in fine fashion, with a jump of 1.94 metres. She continued jumping at the Master's levels. Her 20-year career is the most productive of any Canadian high jumper's. She is now the mother of three and works with her husband, a doctor, at a Vancouver rehabilitation centre.

27

Diane Jones-Konihowski
Pentathlon

Hometown: Saskatoon

DIANE JONES BROKE OUT INTO THE LIMELIGHT IN 1964. She was only in grade 10 when she made the national junior team for the high jump and the javelin. Jones wore Canada's colours every season for the next 16 years.

Diane stayed home to attend university and to work with coach Lyle Sanderson at the University of Saskatchewan. He talked the shy multitalented athlete into trying the pentathlon and Jones started her ascent up the Canadian rankings. In 1970, just 19, she went to the last British Empire Games — they became the Commonwealth Games — in Edinburgh, Scotland.

Two years later Diane was a member of Canada's Olympic team in Munich when 11 Israeli team members, 5 hostage-takers and a German police officer were killed after Palestinian terrorists stormed the Israeli athletes' residence to take hostages. The Israeli team and the Canadian team were neighbours in a dormitory in the Olympic village. The horrible event had a traumatic effect on all the athletes in the village. The Summer Games would never provide Diane's greatest moments.

In 1974 Diane travelled to Christchurch, New Zealand,

for the new Commonwealth Games. Torn ligaments she suffered in a pickup volleyball game forced her to miss out on an anticipated gold-medal battle with the English champion Mary Peters.

The following season Diane was in excellent competition condition and fought her way right into the middle of the world rankings after she set a new world record of 4540 points at the Canadian Indoor Championships. Her gold medal at the Pan Am Games in Mexico City sealed her selection as Canadian Female Athlete of the Year. Diane humbly gave all the credit to her national team coach Bob Adams. She never took credit for anything except the mistakes. That's how she was. Now the Montreal Olympics were straight ahead and "Jonesy" seemed on course for a medal at home.

The pressure on Canada's team going into the summer of 1976 was considerable. Diane was a self-titled "shy prairie girl" when the television cameras found her. It was the biggest media happening in Canadian history and the need for content never went away. Diane spent more time talking to reporters than she should have. She was a tired stressed-out athlete by the time they left her alone.

One press estimate suggested that Diane was the most photographed athlete in Montreal. The sixth-place finishes in front of the huge home crowd left the whole 1976 Olympic experience a hollow one for Diane. She headed home to recuperate.

Diane was determined to learn from her Montreal mistake, and when the Edmonton Commonwealth Games approached in 1978, she ignored the circus and focused on the prize. Her gold-medal performance in front of her friends and family was the best effort and scored the highest point total of any pentathlete in the world that season. Her smile lifted the disappointment of past meets.

Diane was filled with renewed confidence and defended her Pan Am gold in 1979 in Puerto Rico. She entered what would be her final Olympic competition year in the world's top three, giving her a serious shot at a medal in Moscow. For the first time Diane felt that Olympic glory was right there in her grasp.

When the Soviet Union invaded Afghanistan in 1979, the president of the United States, Jimmy Carter, announced that his country would boycott the Moscow Olympics in the summer of 1980. American athletes were shocked. The Olympics only come every four years. A career doesn't offer that many chances. Was a boycott by athletes the solution to anything? Many high-profile U.S. athletes didn't think so and they spoke out in opposition.

After Canada's government chose to support U.S. policy and to get in line with West Germany and Japan, our athletes shared the same shock. To Jones, all the work, all the pain, all the sacrifice seemed to amount to nothing.

For a time, athletes from boycotting countries talked of competing as an independent team. Diane and other Canadian athletes considered the option, but she had no real choice. Her Olympic dream was over along with the entire 1980 Canadian Olympic team's.

The Moscow Summer Olympic Games went on. Records were broken, underdogs came through, great veterans took their final bows.

The boycott served no apparent purpose. The war dragged on for nine more years. The Soviet Union retaliated in 1984 and led a Warsaw Pact boycott of the Los Angeles Summer Olympics.

Two weeks after the Moscow Games Diane Jones defeated both the Olympic gold and silver medallists in a pentathlon meet in Germany. She retired at the end of the season.

Diane married Edmonton Eskimo star wide receiver John Konihowski and stayed active in sports. Their daughter Jana is an elite-level volleyball player. In 2002 Diane served as *chef de mission* for Canada's Olympic team in Sydney, Australia, and in that same year was awarded an honorary degree from her alma mater.

28

The 1976 Montreal Summer Olympic Games

Montreal, Quebec

IN 1970 THE INTERNATIONAL OLYMPIC COMMITTEE convened in Amsterdam to announce the winner of the bid to hold the 1976 Summer Games. The three cities in the running were Los Angeles, Moscow and Montreal. The Games were awarded to Montreal. Mayor Jean Drapeau and his bid team celebrated into the night.

Mayor Drapeau was the driving force behind the acquisition of the Games. Montreal had hosted the world's fair — Expo 67 — which had put the city into the international spotlight. Drapeau loved that spotlight. He had a vision for his city and cost would be no object. His plan would lead to the further revitalization of Montreal — for highways, public transit, sports facilities — and it came to pass. But there were a few obstacles to overcome. And there was a great price tag left in the aftermath.

The first big obstacle occurred at the Munich Games in 1972 when Palestinian extremists took 11 members of Israel's Olympic team hostage. The tense standoff focused world attention on Munich; because all the Israelis were killed, along with five of their captors and a West German police officer, the president of the IOC, Avery Brundage, suggested that the future of the Games was in jeopardy and might never fully recover. It would be up to Montreal to put the lustre back on the Olympic rings.

To help offset the cost of hosting the games, the Montreal Organizing Committee unveiled some innovative programs, and governments at all levels helped out: the Royal Canadian Mint struck commemorative coins, the post office released a special series of stamps and, for the first time in history, a national lottery was made available to the Canadian public. All these programs were successful and the temporary lotteries went on to become permanent features of Canadian life — a whole new way for governments to generate revenue. However, cost overruns have become part of the Canadian fabric. The estimated billion-dollar shortfall in Montreal grew and remains a bone of contention to this day. To many people, the Olympic Games are an economic equation. To others, they are a triumph of the human spirit.

The last big hurdle to cross came as a form of protest. Twenty-six African nations decided to boycott Montreal as a condemnation of the apartheid policies of South Africa. Although that country was banned from taking part in the Games, a rugby team from New Zealand had played a side from South Africa in an exhibition series in the lead up to Montreal. New Zealand was sending a team to Canada, so the African nations decided not to go.

In the end, 92 nations sent 6028 athletes to compete in 21 sports and on July 17 they gathered outside the Olympic Stadium for the opening ceremony and the realization of Jean Drapeau's dream.

Canada's prime minister, Pierre Elliott Trudeau, attended

with his family; U.S. President Jimmy Carter attended with Mrs. Carter; and Her Majesty Queen Elizabeth II brought the royal family and declared the Summer Games of Montreal open. The Olympic flame was sent from Mount Olympus, Greece, as a satellite transmission to trigger a laser that ignited the torch.

Two teenagers, Stéphane Préfontaine and Sandra Henderson, carried the Olympic torch into the packed stadium. They represented the future and lit the Montreal flame to get that future started. By the end of the celebrations, Canadians were basking in rare national pride and the Olympic movement was already breathing new life.

Athletic heroes emerged from every corner of the Olympics. Fourteen-year-old Romanian gymnast Nadia Comaneci scored the first perfect 10.0s ever at the Olympics. Sugar Ray Leonard led the greatest U.S. boxing team of all time into the ring. Cuba's Alberto Juantorena redefined the middle-distance race and Shun Fujimoto became a hero in Japan when he secretly competed in the gymnastics team event on a broken leg so that his fellow countrymen would not be disqualified. His dismount from the rings remains a portrait of athletic courage. It is the heroes who shape each Olympics. They are the Games' most important product, after all. Montreal succeeded in producing a host of international heroes.

Canadian athletic results were disappointing. With five silver medals and six bronze medals, Canada became the first country to ever host the Games without winning gold. But images of Greg Joy at the high jump in the rain, Cheryl Gibson in the pool, John Wood in the C-1 canoe and Michel Vaillancourt on County Branch in the equestrian ring on the final day will always remain great moments for Canada.

For 17 glorious days, Canadian fans stared transfixed at their televisions as Montreal restored the spirit to the Olympic Games. Kids from sea to sea to seas were inspired to take up the Olympic challenge and follow their own dreams.

The real legacy of Montreal was never in the buildings or on the balance sheet but in the swelling ranks of participants at the grassroots level in Olympic sports. The seeds for those sports that Canada became powerful in 20 years later, such as rowing, cycling and athletics, were planted in the summer of 1976.

When the Montreal Olympics drew to a close on August 1, most of the critics had been converted and friends from all around the world had been made. The City of Montreal, like all Olympic host cities, would never be the same.

29

Arnie Boldt
High jumper

Hometown: Saskatoon

IN 1948, 16 BRITISH WORLD WAR II VETERANS WITH spinal cord injuries gathered in the little village of Stoke Mandeville in Buckinghamshire, England, to compete in sport events. Four years later, with athletes from Holland participating, a movement was born. In 1960, the competition was organized like the Olympics and held in Rome just like the Olympics. It was called the Olympiad for the Disabled and there were three hundred participants. Arnie Boldt was three years old that year.

Arnie was born into life on the farm. His family lived near Osler, Saskatchewan. He was an energetic child who loved to be wherever the action was. That usually meant wherever the adults were, which was usually someplace doing chores. Arnie loved to help out with the chores. In the fall of his third year, the little boy suffered a horrible farm accident when his right leg was mangled in a grain auger. The child nearly bled to death. The doctors had to amputate what little was left of the limb.

Arnie adapted. He had no choice really. So he threw himself headlong back into life and tried to be as normal as everyone else.

115

In grade 3 Arnie competed in the school field-day competitions. He tried the high jump and the standing long jump and he had a great day. Soon he was jumping over everything in sight. He made a jump area in the rec room, where he jumped over the couch into piled-up cushions. He built an outdoors pit, using old lumber for stands, and a hay-filled landing pit. Pretty soon the whole community was cheering Arnie on.

While getting a new prosthetic, Arnie learned about organized competitions for amputees. He was already playing wheelchair basketball and volleyball, but he wanted to spend more time focused on track and started winning events around the province. When Toronto hosted the 1976 Olympiad for the Disabled, the organizing committee expanded the competition by adding new events. High jump and the standing long jump, Arnie's specialties, would be on the schedule. And Arnie would be on Canada's team.

Arnie responded in front of the supportive Toronto crowd. First he set a world record in the standing long jump and then the bar in the high jump reached 6 feet and everyone at the meet stopped to watch. Arnie defied gravity that day as he sailed over the bar at 6 feet 1 1/4 inches (1.86 metres) — on one leg and without any formal training. It was an unprecedented athletic achievement and Arnie drew cheers from around the world. At home, he finished second to Greg Joy as Canadian Male Athlete of the Year. Joy won a silver medal that summer at the Montreal Olympics with a jump of 2.23 metres. Arnie's 1.86-metre jump in Toronto just seemed higher somehow.

After Toronto, Arnie went to the University of Saskatchewan and later to the University of Manitoba. He competed on the track team at both schools as a regular varsity athlete. He also travelled to invitational track meets around the world, competing in both abled and disabled events. In Canadian Intercollegiate Athletic Union (CIAU) meets he regularly cleared 2 metres.

Arnie was a pioneer for disabled athletes and he challenged the system to respond to their needs as athletes. Each year he applied for funding and each year he was turned down. It was only in the final two years of Arnie's extraordinary 18-year career that he received any government assistance for sports. When he went to Europe to compete he was a star. At home he was a non-status athlete.

Arnie kept raising the bar and at an indoor meet just before the 1980 outdoor season he cleared 2.04 metres. Since it was a regular meet it didn't count as a disabled record. None of his jumps in regular CIAU competition did, but Arnie felt that competing against the best competition possible was crucial. It made him better.

In 1980 the Olympiad was held in the Netherlands. On a cold wet day in July, Arnie cleared the bar at 1.96 metres — a new world record for disabled athletes. It still stands as the Paralympics record. He added a win in the standing long jump to complete the double-gold performance.

Arnie's best season came the following year. That summer, at a meet in Italy, he won the high jump by clearing 2.04 metres. During the indoor season he competed at the Tribune Games in Winnipeg, and in front of family and friends he cleared 2.08 metres. That jump stood as his personal best in competition.

Arnie kept on jumping far into the 1980s before retiring. He competed through 20 seasons as a world-class athlete.

He kept fighting for recognition for disabled athletes the whole time.

Thanks to work by innovators like Arnie, the movement grew and became the Paralympics. Since 1988 in Seoul, the Paralympics have been held in the Olympic City after the Games. In Atlanta at the 1996 Paralympics Games, Bin Hou of China cleared 1.92 metres. That's the closest anyone's come to Arnie's record.

In 2000 in Sydney nearly 3900 athletes representing 123 nations competed at the Summer Paralympics. The Salt Lake City Winter Paralympics in 2002 drew record crowds.

Arnie Boldt lives with his wife, Inga, and their two children in Thompson, Manitoba. He works at Keewatin Community College.

30

Terry Fox
Runner

Hometown: Port Coquitlam, B.C.

IN ALL OF CANADA'S ATHLETIC HISTORY, ONE STORY STANDS above the rest. It's about a boy who saw that action had to be taken and who, in spite of the cost to him, simply did something — something that made him a man and a true Canadian hero.

Terry Fox wasn't even a particularly good athlete — at least not in the beginning. It's just that he was so determined. Terry played everything as a kid but he loved basketball most of all and he really loved being part of a team. By the time he got to grade 8 he was really bad at the game. But that just made him more determined to get better and to reach his potential.

In high school, basketball coach Bob McGill didn't have the heart to cut Terry. He worked so hard that he stuck with the team. His attitude rubbed off on the other players and that was good for everybody. Terry wasn't a star but he made a positive contribution and coach McGill placed a high value on contribution.

Over the summer Terry played hoops with his pals every day in his spare time. He also picked berries to earn spending money. The teenager was learning the value of money and budgeting at the same time as he was stepping up his defence. That fall the hours on the court paid off and Terry became a starting guard. He started every game throughout the rest of his high school career and was named Co-Athlete of the Year in his final season. The kid who couldn't play became the leader of the team because he gave everything he had every time he played.

Terry graduated from Port Coquitlam High with all As except for one B. He registered at Simon Fraser University in Vancouver and planned to try out for the varsity basketball team. Terry was looking ahead to a career teaching phys-ed and following Bob McGill's excellent example. So he decided to major in kinesiology.

SFU coach Alex Devlin cut players who had better skills than Terry but, like McGill, kept Fox on the team. Nobody outworked him. His fierce determination and desire inspired everyone who came in contact with Fox. He was an excellent team player. Devlin became a Fox fan.

Partway through the season, Terry developed a sore knee that became a constant source of pain. He naturally tried to play through the injury but when simple walking became difficult he had it checked out. The test results shocked everyone. Terry had osteogenic sarcoma — bone cancer. His leg would have to be removed six inches above his right knee. There was no time to waste.

Terry rehabilitated quickly. Six weeks after the amputation he was out relearning golf and shooting hoops with other wheelchair athletes. His leg was gone but Terry was still the same young man — determined and ready to get on with his life. The whole experience showed Terry things he hadn't thought of before. He'd seen children suffering from cancer. He'd seen pain and despair and tragedy. So Terry resolved to do something that would raise money for cancer research and to raise awareness for the cause of cancer patients. He decided to run across Canada. All the way from St. John's, Newfoundland, to British Columbia.

Terry began to train in secret with his childhood pal Doug Alward. He told his mom and dad that he was going to run in the Vancouver marathon so they wouldn't worry too much. After 18 months and 5000 warm-up kilometres, Terry shared his plan with his parents. His dream was to raise one dollar from every Canadian — all 23 million of them — for cancer research. He was unshakeable in his vision, so with his parents' blessing Terry headed east toward the sunrise.

On April 12, 1980, Terry dipped his artificial foot into St. John's Harbour and then turned west and started to run. Doug Alward drove the support vehicle, a donated Ford van with a "Marathon of Hope" graphic on the side.

Terry ran 42 kilometres a day, rain or shine. That's a full marathon every day on an artificial leg. At first the going was tough. The Marathon of Hope's visibility was still low. Donations were few; no one knew that he was even out there running. But Terry kept going and the news started to spread. He ran across PEI and through Nova Scotia, New Brunswick and Quebec. The people were coming out to see the kid with the dream, and the donations were piling up. By the time he hit Toronto in the heat of the summer everybody in the country knew Terry Fox. He was touching hearts and inspiring people. By the time he left Southern Ontario the whole world knew about his courageous run.

Terry Fox and the Marathon of Hope passed through

Sudbury, Ontario, in mid-August. Terry was at the midway point of his journey and happy to have the big Eastern cities behind him.

On September 1 Terry experienced chest pains and breathing difficulties that forced him to stop running for the first time on the journey. Everyone around Terry knew that it must be serious. He had covered 5373 kilometres in 143 days since St. John's to the spot near Thunder Bay at the side of the Trans-Canada Highway where he left the course. Terry left for B.C. and the counsel of his doctors.

The diagnosis was conclusive. The cancer had spread to Terry's lungs. His marathon was over but the donations kept coming. The impression he made was so strong that people just kept giving. The total reached $24.2 million. Even more than he'd dreamed.

Terry fox died on June 28, 1981, a month short of his 23rd birthday in June of 1981. But his message was not buried with his body. Terry's dream travelled around the globe. Each year Terry Fox Runs are held in cities all over the world. More than $340 million has been raised in his honour for the benefit of cancer research.

31

Victor Davis
Swimming

———

Hometown: Guelph, Ontario

VICTOR DAVIS LIVED HIS SHORT, BRILLIANT LIFE WITH A motto in mind: Go big or go home. Victor always went big.

Victor started at age eight. And he was fast and gritty even then. Once he was old enough, Victor joined his hometown Guelph Marlins Swim Club and became the dominant swimmer in the area in his favourite discipline, the breaststroke. Next, he moved over to the Region of Waterloo Swim Club and kept on winning, which naturally caught the attention of the national team coaches. They called Victor to join the big team when he was just 17 years old. Victor was the youngest male swimmer in Canada's history to ever make the national team.

In 1982 Victor went to Brisbane, Australia, for his first big international swim meet — the Commonwealth Games — in the red and white colours of Canada. He and his fellow Canadian swimmers tossed red-and-white Frisbees to the big Australian crowd. The team from Oz had long been one of Canada's biggest swimming rivals. Victor delighted the team and his long-time coach Clifford Barry with a gold medal in the 200-metre breaststroke and silver in the 100-metre distance.

Davis's unforgettable intensity made a deep impression on the many fans that watched him swim. He was disappointed in himself because he felt that winning was the only option. During the 4 × 100-metre individual-medley relay, his intensity boiled over and he kicked a plastic chair across the pool deck. The Games featured many royal spectators and that was the case during this race. The sliding chair drew anxious looks from the gathered officials but it was just Davis. That's the way he was. Victor's reputation as the bad boy of the pool grew that day. But so did Canada's medal haul. At so many meets he lived up to his name — Victor. At so many medal ceremonies he stood victorious.

He then went to the World Championships in Ecuador and repeated his victories — gold and a new world record at 200 metres and silver at 100 metres.

Victor struck up a strong friendship with his teammate, individual-medley specialist Alex Baumann of Sudbury. Alex's calm, easygoing ways were the perfect balance to Victor's fiery tempestuous nature. Together they led Canada's greatest Olympic swim team into the Summer Games of Los Angeles in 1984.

The L.A. Games were boycotted by the Soviet Union and its allies in retaliation for the Moscow Olympics boycott of 1980, which had been led by the USA. But the effect on the swim meet was marginal, if any. Los Angeles featured the three strongest men's teams in the world that year by far — Australia, Canada and the home-favoured U.S. team. These traditional aquatic rivals produced one of the most exciting swim meets in Olympic history. Alex won two gold medals while Victor contributed silver in the 100-metre breaststroke and gold in the 200-metre event. He broke his own world record with the gold-medal performance. Then, as a member of Canada's 4 x 100-metre medley-relay team with Tom Ponting, Michael West and Sandy Goss, Victor contributed a second silver medal performance. Go big or go home. Canadian fans were overjoyed.

At the 1986 Commonwealth Games in Edinburgh, Scotland, Victor finished second in the 200-metre breaststroke. The relay team with Victor swimming the breaststroke leg won Scottish gold.

The World Championships that year were held in Madrid, Spain, and Victor turned his usual pattern around by winning silver in the 200-metre breaststroke and gold in the 100. Still, he was the dominant swimmer on the planet in his discipline.

In 1987 Victor lowered his personal best 200-metre distance time set in L.A. in 1984 and established a new Canadian record that stood until 2002. The record produced one of the 31 national titles that Victor held during his career.

Victor led a new generation of swimmers to Seoul in 1988. His fourth-place finish in the 100-metre breaststroke kept him off the podium, but the veteran teamed up with Mark Tewksbury, Tom Ponting and Sandy Goss to bring Canada a bronze medal in the 4 x 100-metre medley relay. Victor watched his beloved Red Leaf fly over an Olympic medal ceremony one last time.

In the fall of 1988 Victor called his career complete and retired. He figured it was time to move on and find another career. In November 1989 a few weeks later, he was run down while on foot in Montreal's West End by a driver that he'd had an argument with only moments earlier. As Victor

Davis lay dying in the hospital, his parents courageously decided that their son's organs should help people in need. Victor's kidneys, his liver and his heart were transplanted immediately into waiting recipients. His corneas went to the Montreal Eye Bank. In the end, Victor gave life to others. That's big.

Today Victor's large legend still touches Canadian swimming — his sport. The Victor Davis Memorial Fund provides financial aid and bursaries for up-and-coming swimmers who face financial hardships. His parents have asked that Victor's fans consider signing organ donor cards in their son's memory.

32

Sylvie Fréchette
Synchro swimming

Hometown: Montreal

SYLVIE FRÉCHETTE WAS ONLY THREE YEARS OLD WHEN HER dad died. Mme. Fréchette was left alone in Montreal with her two children. She was determined to make a good life for Sylvie and her baby brother and supported her children at every turn. Nothing came easy.

Sylvie joined the Aquatic Club of Montreal when she was eight and synchronized swimming became her passion. Early success at competitions attracted the attention of Julie Sauvé, who became Sylvie's lifelong coach. In 1979 the coach took her star athlete to the Canadian Junior Championships where she placed 19th in the duet. The coach reminded Sylvie that she'd need patience and grace to get to the top of the sport. Two years later, barely in her teens, Sylvie won gold in the solo and gold in the duet. The road to the top looked long and wide open in front of her. All she'd have to do is work hard and wait for her moment of glory.

In 1983, Sylvie became a member of Canada's national team. She climbed quickly to the top of the World Junior rankings and won competitions in pools all around the world. With Carolyn Waldo and Michelle Cameron in front of her at the senior level, all Sylvie had to do was compete, learn and be patient. Sylvie was up to the task.

At the 1986 Edinburgh Commonwealth Games, Sylvie won gold for Canada in the solo event and then, as a member of the synchro team, shared gold at the World Championships later in the summer at Madrid, Spain. Because the team event was not on the schedule for the Seoul Olympics in 1988, Sylvie sat out and watched Waldo win gold in the solo and then win another with Cameron in the duet. As the anthem played for Canada's synchro stars, Sylvie knew her turn was next.

By the time the Auckland, New Zealand, Commonwealth Games rolled around in 1990, Sylvie was in her own class as a synchronized swimmer. She received the first-ever perfect scores of 10 at that meet. At the World Championships that followed, she set a record for total combined score — 203.013 — it still stands. A year later she was the undisputed solo World Cup Champion and the World Champion. She would leave for Barcelona in 1992 as the odds-on favourite to win Olympic gold. That's the way it looked anyway.

Sylvie never shied away from hard work. During the lead-up year before the Olympics she finished her bachelor's degree at l'Université de Montréal. As if that wasn't quite enough, Sylvie became engaged to be married and life looked like a cruise. After that, the road steepened.

A few months before Sylvie was scheduled to leave for Europe, her grandfather died. Then, one week before her Olympic trip, she arrived home to discover her fiancé had committed suicide. Sylvie's entire world was torn to shreds.

Sylvie decided to carry on. It's what she best knew how to do. She'd make the journey to Barcelona with her coach and her supporters and join her team to compete for her country. The pain and grief would have to wait.

Sylvie's swim in Barcelona's beautiful outdoors pool was simply magnificent — a gold-medal performance by any measure. The stirring music and Sylvie's magnetism brought the fans to their feet; all the emotion that she had inside during that time came out in the performance. The crowd rose to its feet at the finish. But when her marks were totalled there was something terribly wrong. Sylvie sat in silence as the story unfolded.

The judge from Panama entered a score of 8.7 instead of the 9.7 she'd intended. However, the head judge let the marks stand. Sylvie was awarded a silver medal. Gold went to Kristen Babb-Sprague of the USA. It was a terrible injustice.

When the Games drew to a close, Dick Pound, then vice-president of the International Olympic Committee, launched an investigation and an appeal on Sylvie's behalf. Pound, a fellow Montrealer, swam for Canada in 1960 at Rome. Sylvie waited patiently. Something she knew how to do.

Thanks to Pound's tenacity, justice finally prevailed and Sylvie's gold medal was presented 16 months later at the packed Montreal Forum. In that moment, Sylvie Fréchette redefined the concepts of grace and dignity in sports. Pound appropriately presented her with the gold medal. Sylvie retired after what she called the happiest day of her life. She had it coming.

Sylvie took time off to re-evaluate what she wanted to do with her life. She retired from competition and took on speaking engagements, a television interview program called *Simplement Sylvie* and a public relations position with the

National Bank of Canada. But she missed the competition and the events. She missed the show. She even missed the practice. And she especially missed the creative rush of building a program. So when Canada's team needed a stabilizing influence in 1996 to be part of the national team, Sylvie answered the call. The veteran helped Canada to a silver medal in the team competition at the Atlanta Olympics. Her competitive career came to an end with Canada's flag on the silver pole at the medal ceremony. She was content.

Sylvie moved forward with her life. She married and developed a career as a world-renowned choreographer and aquatic designer. She created a masterpiece for Quebec's own Cirque du Soleil and designed their thrilling Las Vegas show "O."

33

Lennox Lewis
Boxing

———◦◦◦◦———

Hometown: Kitchener, Ontario

ONE OF THE GREATEST WISHES OF VETERAN ATHLETES, particularly the great ones, is to have the wisdom to seize the right moment to retire: To go out on top. Sadly, most wait too long. Lennox Lewis got it just right.

Lennox was born in 1965 in London, England's, tough East End. His mom and dad split up when Lennox was still a child. Mrs. Lewis decided to leave the harsh streets of London and to travel to Canada. She landed a job in Kitchener, Ontario, and set about raising her son in a safer environment. Lennox thrived and grew.

At school, Lennox played basketball, football — everything. He was fluid and fast and big. He started training with Arnie Boehm and Hook McComb at the Kitchener–Waterloo Regional Boxing Association, the same club where future light heavyweight champion Donny Lalonde started out. Because Lewis was so large, he had to stand in against smaller, faster fighters. Lennox developed quick hands.

In 1983 Lennox made his first mark on the international boxing scene when he won the World Junior Championship as a member of Canada's boxing team. In 1984 the teenager gained valuable international experience and felt the emotional rush of patriotism when his fellow national boxing team members, Willie Dewitt, Sean O'Sullivan and Dale Walters, won medals at the Los Angeles Olympics. He wanted one of his own.

Four years later at the 1988 Seoul Olympics, Lennox fought his way into the final. He'd have to face the heavily favoured U.S. champion, Riddick Bowe, for the super heavyweight gold medal. But all of this was lost in the aftermath of Ben Johnson's steroid bust. Johnson won the 100-metre sprint in world record time and the country went wild. A few days later Ben tested positive and was stripped of the medal. Canada's pride went with it. We desperately needed a hero to step up for us. Lennox did just that and won a big chunk of our dignity back when he demolished the Bowe for the gold medal. He became Canada's first Olympic boxing champion since 1932, when Horace Left Gwynne won gold as a bantamweight.

When Lennox turned professional, he returned to the city of his birth to establish his base. In London, Lennox was able to develop away from the spotlight and he worked hard to improve his skills. Though roundly criticized by members of the Canadian press for the move, it was the perfect thing for Lennox to do. In England, he'd be able to develop out of the media's glare. At 6 feet 5 inches and 250 pounds, he piled up the victories in Europe.

Then in 1992 Lennox destroyed fellow Canadian Razor Ruddock in London to earn a shot at the WBC Championship against his old Olympic foe Riddick Bowe. But Bowe refused to fight Lennox and chose to throw the WBC into a garbage can at a press conference. Lennox was awarded the championship belt by default. One of the first things he did with the prize money was to build a new house for his mom in Brampton, Ontario.

Lennox became the first British heavyweight champion in more than a hundred years and the first Canadian to hold the belt since Tommy Burns was champ 90 years earlier. He beat Tony Tucker in his first title defence in 1993. But the press was slow to acknowledge his skill.

Lennox took on all viable challengers. He lost his grip on the heavyweight title just two times through the span — once in September 1994 to Oliver McCall and once to Hasim Rahman in April 2001. Neither was highly regarded and Lennox defeated both by knockouts in rematches to get his titles back. The whole time Lennox was fighting in the ring he was also fighting criticism from the media, particularly from the U.S. media, and the champ went on a crusade to change the minds of the skeptics.

In 1999 he fought a rematch with Evander Holyfield after their first bout was called a draw. The winner would wear all of the heavyweight crowns and become the undisputed heavyweight champion of the world. Lewis fans felt the fight was pointless because Lennox had punished Holyfield so badly during their first fight in 1997. But the judges called it a draw, so Lennox beat Holyfield up all over again and unified the title for the first time in years.

In June 2002 in Memphis, Tennessee, Lennox fought former champion Mike Tyson in a long-anticipated match that had been delayed many times. Lennox thoroughly destroyed Tyson and scored an eight-round knockout. Lennox reached the highest point of his storied career right there.

The final out for Lewis came on June 21, 2003, when he stopped Vitali Klitschko of Ukraine on a technical knockout. The doctor at ringside declared the fight over when a Lewis punch opened a huge cut over Klitschko's eye. Lennox's record stood at 41 wins, 2 losses and 1 draw.

When Lennox announced his retirement at a press conference in London early in 2004, he joined Gene Tunney (1928) and Rocky Marciano (1956) as the only heavyweights in history to retire as reigning World Champions. He had won over the doubters and was widely regarded as a great champion and a great gentleman. He retired on top. Perfect ending.

The last words Lennox Lewis spoke as champion were, "Let the next era begin."

34

Ben Johnson
Sprinter

Hometown: Toronto

CANADIAN OLYMPIC SPRINT FANS SUFFERED THROUGH A long, dry spell in the time before Ben. In fact, Ben Johnson wasn't even three years old in 1964 when the great Harry Jerome won bronze for Canada at the Tokyo Olympics. But Ben turned the sprint world into a Canadian oasis — for a while.

The Johnson family emigrated from Falmouth, Jamaica, to Toronto in 1976. Ben was 15. The only thing he liked about high school was track practice and the time he spent with his coach, Percy Duncan. Ben progressed up the national sprint ladder.

In 1981 after the Canadian Track and Field Championships Ben spoke to coach Charlie Francis of the fabled York track team. Francis did not hesitate to recommend, right at the start, the illegal course that would eventually wreck the talented kid's career. He bluntly told Ben that hard work, dedication and steroids were the tried and true way to get to the very top of the sprint world. If Ben wanted to get there, Francis knew how and who. Ben was 19. All he wanted was to get there. A few days later, he decided to work with coach Francis at York and to start on a steroid program.

Ben's rise was rapid after that. His first big international meet was the World Championships in 1983, where he advanced all the way to the semifinals. A year later he made it into the final at the Los Angeles Olympics and surprised everyone with a bronze run behind Carl Lewis's gold-medal performance.

There are a lot of great sprinters in the world and usually it takes many seasons to get to the Olympic podium. Not for Ben. His bronze in L.A. was Canada's first sprint medal since Jerome in 1964. Ben added a bronze in the 4 × 100-metre relay and fans at home started to believe. It felt too good to be true.

Partway through the 1985 season Ben beat Carl Lewis — four-time gold medallist at the L.A. Games — for the first time in seven tries. Their races were like fistfights and their feelings for each other were never hidden. Up to this point it had been Lewis's world, and King Carl walked with attitude in every step.

The fierce rivalry's momentum swung Ben's way in the 1987 season, and at the World Championships in Rome he blew Lewis and the field away with a world record run of 9.83. Canadian fans declared the king was dead, long live the king. Our Ben looked unbeatable.

In the post-race media frenzy after the Rome race, Carl Lewis suggested that a certain sprint gold medallist — he never said Ben's name outright — was taking steroids. There was no positive test to back him up and everybody knows the first three finishers are always tested. The acrimony between Johnson and Lewis intensified.

In February of 1988, the Olympic year, Ben injured his hamstring. Coach Francis and the doctor who administered

Ben's steroid program, Dr. Jamie Astaphan of St. Kitts, saw no need to alter the plan. Just let it heal naturally. Nobody wanted to risk varying from the scientific safety of the program so close to the Olympics.

In May Ben re-injured the hamstring. His support team began to worry when Ben's healing dragged on. Their concern grew when Carl Lewis ran 9.99 in a Paris meet in June. In August the adversaries met for the first time that season and Carl left Ben in his dust. Carl was first, Ben was third and panic was swirling through the Johnson camp. It burst when Ben finished third behind U.S. runners Dennis Mitchell and Calvin Smith in Cologne, Germany. That's when the program was scrapped.

Johnson headed for the Caribbean and St. Kitts before leaving for Seoul and the Olympics. Dr. Astaphan emphasized to Ben and Francis that a dose of steroids so close to the Games would be dangerous and easily detected by the tests in Seoul. The sprinter and his coach ignored the warning and Astaphan administered the steroids. They'd try to mask it somehow.

In Seoul Ben advanced through the heats but not without causing concern. He lined up for the final beside Canadian teammate Desai Williams. Lewis, Smith and Mitchell of the USA, Linford Christie of Great Britain, Ray Lewis of Jamaica and Rob Da Silva of Brazil rounded out the field. Ben was last into the blocks.

It was over in 9.79 seconds. He crushed his existing record. After 47 blazing strides Ben finished 3 full metres in front of Lewis. Christie was third. The entire country rose in unison. Ben wrapped himself in a flag. It was called the September to remember. When Ben got his gold medal,

Canadians were filled up. That was our guy up there, the "world's fastest human." Then it all crashed.

Ben's joy was shattered two-and-a-half days after his greatest triumph by a knock on his hotel-room door. The IOC had come for his gold medal. Ben's post-race urine sample tested positive for an anabolic steroid. Carl Lewis was award gold, Linford Christie moved up to silver, and Dennis Mitchell would gain the bronze. Ben fled Seoul in disgrace.

His world record from Rome was, like his gold medal, stricken from the books. He was suspended for two years.

At the government-sanctioned Dubin Inquiry into athlete drug use in Canada Ben, after initially lying, finally admitted to his mistake. The Inquiry recommended, among other things, better drug testing.

Any sympathy Ben gained through his banishment vanished when he tested positive again in 1993 at a meet in Montreal. Ben was banned for life.

Carl Lewis, Dennis Mitchell and Linford Christie all went on in subsequent years to test positive for banned substances. The use of performance-enhancing drugs has remained rooted in the big-money world of sprinting.

Ben's Seoul time of 9.79 wasn't equalled until 2002 when U.S. sprinter Tim Montgomery posted a new world mark of 9.78 seconds.

35

Mark McKoy
Hurdles

Hometown: Toronto

MARK MCKOY KNOCKED DOWN A LOT OF HURDLES ON HIS way to Olympic gold, but he never gave up or quit trying, even when the road grew steep.

The McKoy family moved from Georgetown, Guyana, to Toronto in 1973. Mark was 12, a difficult age for a boy to leave his friends.

In high school, Mark's natural speed led him to the track team. Before long he was the fastest hurdler in Ontario. By 1980 he was a member of the national team and training year-round. In 1982 he won the gold medal for Canada at the Commonwealth Games. He wasn't even 21 yet. In nine years he'd come from being a lonely immigrant kid to the Commonwealth Champion. It was a lot to take in.

In 1984 at the Los Angeles Olympics Mark placed fourth in the hurdles final and he felt disappointed. He just assumed he'd keep moving up. He took some time off to regroup and set new goals. Then he broke back onto the international stage in 1986 in Edinburgh where he defended his Commonwealth Games' gold medal. The win warmed Mark because he beat a strong field that included Colin Jackson of Wales. Six days later, Mark ran lead-off for

Canada's 4 × 100-metre relay team won another gold medal with them. Mark came home proud.

In 1987 Mark stumbled to seventh place at the World Championships. Once again, he'd failed to step up to the front of the class at a big world event. He went looking for reasons why before the Summer Olympics of Seoul in 1988. There were none to be found.

In South Korea Mark worked through the heats and into the final. Then he crashed into the last three hurdles and finished seventh. It was no improvement over his World Championships time. Mark felt stuck on a plateau with no way off. Then everything crashed.

The spirit of the Olympic Games was shattered on the last Tuesday in September 1988. In the early hours of the morning a delegation from the International Olympic Committee went to Ben Johnson's hotel room and stripped him of his gold medal. The 100-metre race he'd won on Saturday was forfeited. Johnson's urine sample tested positive for a banned substance. The party was over.

The track team was coming apart at the seams. Johnson left Seoul. Coaches were leaving the Olympics. Mark, who was supposed to run on Canada's relay team, made a rash decision and flew out of the Olympic City to return home. So began the darkest time in the history of Canadian sport.

In the aftermath of what became the Ben Johnson steroid scandal, Mark admitted to using illegal steroids for a short time. He tried the drug while training at the same club as Ben Johnson with coach Charlie Francis before Seoul. He said he stopped right away because the steroids made him sick. The admission came in testimony given by Mark to the government-ordered Dubin Inquiry into the use of drugs in sport. When the Inquiry was over, Mark served a two-year suspension. He qualified for his real estate licence and tried to eke out a living in a serious market downturn. Nothing was going right for Mark. But he was patient.

The old Iron Curtain divided the former Communist Eastern European countries from the rest of Europe. It was mostly steel fences and razor wire, but in Berlin it was a big concrete wall. That wall seemed to divide the world. When it came down in 1990, Mark's life changed dramatically. He was finally able to be with the woman he loved. Yvette was an East German athlete he'd met after the Los Angeles Olympics. She was unable to travel except to compete so they carried on a secret romance for years in spite of the wall between them. The affair was dangerous for Yvette who was under the constant watch of the Stasi — the East German secret police. But that changed when the wall came down.

Their marriage helped anchor Mark who was training in Wales with his friend and rival, Colin Jackson. With Yvette safe and sound, he began to work even harder. He had a goal now. He had a future. Mark made a quiet return to competition at a meet late in the 1990 season in Montreal, after serving his suspension. He easily reclaimed his Canadian Championship in the 110-metre hurdles. His relay days were over.

At the World Championships a year later in the summer of 1991, Mark downed a double shot of espresso coffee and then went out and placed fourth in the finals. It was an excellent performance for his first major meet in three years. The tide was turning at last.

The 1992 season was perfect from the start. Mark reeled off six consecutive personal-best performances and steadily lowered his Canadian record to 13.11 seconds. He travelled to Barcelona more confident than he'd ever been.

The big moment came on August 3 at the Main Olympic Stadium on Mont Juic. Mark won his semifinal in 13.12 seconds. Later in the day he stepped into the Olympic light for the last time. He walked to the starting area with the other runners, including his friend Colin Jackson, who ran for Great Britain. The crowd hushed and Mark got set in the blocks. He focused directly on hurdle number one. The gun sounded and 13.12 seconds later Mark was the Olympic gold-medal champion. Even though he hit the last hurdle, he kept going — he just never gave up.

Mark won Canada's first gold medal in Olympic men's track and field competition in 64 years — the first since Percy Williams won twice in 1928. The medal ceremony and playing of Canada's anthem helped ease the pain of Seoul.

Mark and Yvette are the proud parents of two children, a daughter and a son.

Curt Harnett
Cycling

Hometown: Thunder Bay, Ontario

CURT HARNETT WENT TO HIS FOURTH AND FINAL OLYMPIC competition in Atlanta in 1996. He carried a simple message that became the rallying cry of the entire Canadian Olympic team: Let's kick some butt. The blond warrior did just that on the velodrome at Stone Mountain, Georgia, when he met and beat his career-long archrival Gary Neiwand of Australia for the bronze medal. Curt called it a career right after the medal ceremony. His message stuck.

Curt grew up in Thunder Bay and was, like most of the guys he knew, passionate about hockey. Curt had a great shot and, at 6 feet and 220 pounds, he never backed off when the games got rough. In the summer he took to the bicycle to help stay in shape, but hockey was the dream he was chasing as a teenager.

Curt got all the way to junior and was trying out for an Ontario Hockey League team before he realized that his true calling wasn't in the arena at all but rather out on the road riding a bike — fast. At 16, when the wins started piling up at races around the Lakehead, he threw himself headlong into cycling, and Canada found a new two-wheeled champion.

By 1982 Curt became a member of the national team and competed at the Pan Am Games in Caracas, Venezuela, the following year. No one felt prouder wearing Canada's colours. He placed fourth in the 1000-metre time trials and cemented his spot on the bike squad for the 1984 Los Angeles Olympic Games.

At L.A. Curt finished second in the time-trial event and proudly watched Canada's flag being raised at the medal ceremony. He held his head high and stood tall, the silver medal hanging from his neck. With his long blond hair and great big smile, Curt caught the nation's eye.

In 1986 the Commonwealth Games were held in Edinburgh, Scotland, and Curt switched disciplines to the most powerful of all cycling track events — the match sprint. The sprint is a head-to-head race that brings strategy and the mental game into the picture. Curt loved the challenge of the velodrome boards. He placed fifth in Scotland in his first big sprint test.

Then Curt went on in 1987 to win gold at the Indianapolis Pan Am Games in the 1000-metre time trial and bronze in the match sprint. In a sport of specialists, Curt had a choice to make. Curt, who always believed in following his heart, turned his back on the 1000-metre event in favour of the more strategic match-sprint race.

In Seoul in 1988, Harnett hoped to move up the sprint ladder but he finished 10th. Rather than return to the time trial, Curt stepped up his commitment and his focus and went to work with coach Roger Young on a whole new fitness and nutrition program. Curt's thighs, always large, grew to powerful proportions in the weight room. He trained year-round in Southern California and he studied the art of match racing at every opportunity that he could.

In 1990 Curt had his breakthrough season. At the Auckland Commonwealth Games meet in New Zealand he placed second to the Australian Neiwand, his archrival. That season he also placed second at the World Championships in Japan and won gold at Seattle's Goodwill Games while placing first in two World Cup events. Curt stood, with a handful of riders, as the best in the sport.

The 1992 Olympic Games in Barcelona saw Curt standing on the medal podium with Jens Fieldler of Germany and Gary Neiwand of Australia ahead of him. Curt was on the bronze step. He ached for a velodrome rematch with Neiwand.

Curt's chance came at home in 1994 at Victoria's Commonwealth Games. The two rivals worked their way through the heats and into the final. The gold-medal match-up was a classic race, but Neiwand prevailed and Curt settled for silver. He held his head high once again.

The year 1995 brought Curt's 30th birthday. He knew that his athletic career was entering its final phase. Although he ended up with the silver medal in the 200-metre sprint at the World Championships at Bogota, Colombia, he set a world record in the 200-metre sprint-qualifying rounds to become the first man to go under 10 seconds (9.865). He wrapped up that season by finishing in second place at the World Championship. The 1996 Olympics in Atlanta were looming. He knew they would be his last Summer Games.

Curt tuned up for the Atlanta Olympics by posting victories at World Cup races in Athens and Milan. He happily served as the leader of a Canadian cycling team that was becoming a force in the sport. Most of all he wanted one more shot at Gary Neiwand. It came in the July heat of Georgia in the bronze-medal match race.

Before the racing events even began, Curt became Captain Canada to the Olympic team with his "kick butt" message. He figured that Canadian athletes needed to step up and realize that they were as good as any in the world. He was right. Our Atlanta team responded and on July 29 he had the chance to contribute to Canada's medal haul. The only obstacle standing in his way was Gary Neiwand of Australia.

Curt caught Neiwand by surprise and dipped down the velodrome wall at Stone Mountain. He blasted underneath the startled Australian on the last lap of their last match race. Then, with his legs furiously pumping, Curt began the final sprint to the finish of his great career. At the wire, it was Canada for bronze and Curt was happy.

In 14 years as a Canadian team member, Curt held more than 30 national titles and in Atlanta he was able to make a decision most athletes only dream of making: Curt Harnett retired on top.

His message still resonates with the national team.

37

Mark Tewksbury
Swimming

─────◦◦◦◦◦─────

Hometown: Calgary

MARK TEWKSBURY WAS JUST FIVE YEARS OLD WHEN HIS DAD was transferred from Calgary to Dallas, Texas, for a two-year company posting. To beat the heat, the family took to the swimming pool. Mark felt right at home in the water, so his parents signed him up for a local Dallas swim club, where he started to work on the basics. A gold-medal career was launched.

The Tewksburys aimed the moving van north after the two-year task was done and drove home to Calgary. Mark registered at the Cascade Swim Club. Before too long he was the best backstroker in the Bow Valley.

Mark moved up to the high-performance team at the University of Calgary and coach Deryk Snelling, one of the very best in the world. By 1985 the 17-year-old Mark was on the national team. Over the next seven seasons, "Tewks" set 21 Canadian records — 11 individually and 10 as a member of various relay teams.

By the end of that first season, Mark's world ranking in the 100-metre backstroke went from 54 to 4. He and Snelling were on the same page and Mark was brimming with confidence in his ability in the pool.

In 1986 Mark was a member of Canada's outstanding Commonwealth Games swim team. Alex Baumann, Victor Davis and Mark led a Canadian aquatic assault at the pool in Scotland. Mark won gold in his individual event, the 100-metre backstroke and with the 4 x 100-metre medley relay team in Edinburgh. Canadian-team Frisbees filled the air at the medal ceremonies.

Mark's fourth-place finish at the World Championships in the 100-metre backstroke final that year kept him right at the top level of the sport. But he was still a step below the podium. Mark would need to find some more speed for the already quick 100-metre trip down the pool and back again.

In 1987 Mark turned 20 and turned up his program. By the end of the season, he was ranked second in the world. The 1988 Olympics in Seoul, South Korea, would provide his ultimate challenge and Tewksbury felt ready to meet it head on.

Many of the elite swimmers in the world chose the Olympic year to switch over to the new underwater dolphin kick in the backstroke. The mermaid-motion of the dolphin kick allowed them to stay under water and generate more power off the turn. Mark made the last-minute decision to stick with the conventional flutter-kick style. It cost him dearly and he slipped to fifth place in the 100-metre final. Some of the disappointment was erased in the 4 x 100-metre medley final when he swam the lead-off backstroke leg for Canada and won a bronze medal with Victor Davis, Tom Ponting and Sandy Goss. Still, Mark came home hurting from Seoul.

Mark resolved to fight on for another four years. He converted to the dolphin kick and his times began to come down. In 1990 Mark went to Auckland, New Zealand, to successfully defend his Commonwealth Games gold medals. Then a year later he hooked up in a thrilling race with Jeff Rouse of the USA at the World Championships and finished second to the American in the final. The margin of victory was .006 seconds and Mark resolved to close it before the Olympics in 1992.

In the lead-up season before the Barcelona Games Tewksbury sought out the guidance of fellow Calgarian Debbie Muir. Debbie coached at Calgary's famous Belles Synchronized Swimming Club. She guided Carolyn Waldo to solo gold in Seoul and then helped Waldo and Michelle Cameron win gold in the duet event. Gold was the colour that most interested Mark, who was looking to refine his dolphin kick.

In Barcelona in 1992 the dolphin kick was working beautifully and Mark moved through the heats and toward the inevitable showdown with his American rival. In the big race, Mark was relaxed and focused. Rouse broke out at the start and held his lead to the turn. Then Mark's all-new-and-improved dolphin kick powered him to the come-from-behind victory. He just edged out Jeff Rouse at the wall to become the Olympic 100-metre backstroke gold medallist. David Berkhoff of the USA captured the bronze medal. Mark raised his arms in victory in his lane at the end of the pool.

Mark's unbridled joy touched a big audience. Canada stood with him for the medal ceremony and playing of "O Canada." Tears streamed down Mark's face as the Red Leaf rose higher than the silver- and bronze-medal flags of the USA.

Mark came home energized, resolved to carry his love of the Olympics in a new direction. He worked with both the Canadian Olympic Association and the International Olympic Association in various roles before taking some time off to reflect on his life.

In 1995 Mark moved to Australia to complete his degree in Political Science. A year later he returned home to resume his role with the IOC but quit in disgust when the Salt Lake Olympic bid committee bribery scandals came to light.

Mark moved forward and co-founded the OATH (Olympic Advocates Honourably Together) movement. The organization aims to raise awareness for and directly help fund athletes in need through training rough spots. He is an avid crusader for Aids Awareness and Prevention.

38

Donny Lalonde
Light heavyweight champion of the world

--- ∞ ---

Hometown: Winnipeg

THE ONE THING DONNY LALONDE NEEDED MOST AS A BOY was a strong male role model. But that wasn't meant to be. Donny was only six in the early 1960s when his parents split up and his dad left the family — his mom, sister and two brothers tried to move on. A few years later when his mom remarried, life looked good.

But Donny and his stepfather just never connected. As time passed, Donny became the object of anger and a victim of child abuse that was so bad the boy was left bleeding and bruised on more than one occasion. The Lalonde brothers were angry, but they were trapped. And no one stepped in.

It was a horrible situation, but Donny and his brothers John and Dash hung together through thick and thin. And they found purpose and motivation at the local boxing gym in Kitchener, Ontario — the same place where Lennox Lewis started his path toward the heavyweight championship of the world. It was a good gym.

The trainers, Hook McComb and Arnie Boehm, gave the boys some direction and they stressed self-discipline. The Lalonde boys quit smoking and started to train seriously. Donny was fearless in the ring — and he packed some serious hurt in his right hand. Opponents who didn't take the long-haired blond kid from Kitchener seriously always paid a heavy price. The wins piled up.

When their mom moved to Winnipeg, the boys found a new gym where Donny and John did the boxing while Dash worked the corner. Soon enough, the Lalonde boys were attracting some attention, and one-time Canadian light heavyweight champion Al Sparks took Donny under his wing. After that, things began to turn around rapidly.

Donny challenged for Rowdy Roddy McDowell's Canadian light heavyweight title. Donny rocked the champ and walked away with the belt. The pride of Winnipeg — the "Golden Boy" — had arrived.

The only way to go was up and the only way to do that was to head south to the big U.S. gyms. So Donny left for Indianapolis where he'd be able to get the training and work he'd need. Donny knew he'd have to put in a lot of training rounds if he were to climb up the ladder in the no-mercy world of professional boxing — which is exactly what he wanted to do.

Donny's crossroads bout was against a very tough opponent named Mustafa Hamsho on May 7, 1987, in New York City at Madison Square Garden. It was pure combat — a bloody war. But Donny prevailed and won the fight in a 12-round decision. He'd been through much worse already in his life, and he was now in line for a shot at the title.

Donny's manager David Wolfe set up the light heavyweight championship title bout with Eddie Davis of the USA. The fight would take place in Trinidad late in 1987. While Donny was prepping for the fight, he trained with

Tommy Galagher at Sullivan's storied gym in Manhattan, the same place Joe Louis trained — a place of champions. During training, the tragic story of an abused child splashed across New York City headlines: the victim, a young girl, had been beaten to death by her parents, both lawyers. It was a horrible incident!

The heartbreaking story of abuse and parental betrayal affected Donny in the most profound way possible. He went to Battery Park to cry. He stared at the water and confronted his own demons. Then he stepped into a new spotlight. He called a press conference and revealed his own abused past. He vowed to dedicate his title fight and all his fights from that point on to abused kids everywhere. It was time someone stepped forward to be their champion. That someone was Donny Lalonde.

Finally, there was a celebrity courageous enough to carry the banner for children suffering at the hands of the people who should love them the most — their parents. But these were parents who'd become the very worst kind of bullies! The whole issue of child abuse was in the open and under discussion. Donny Lalonde helped make that happen.

In Port of Spain, Trinidad, the Golden Boy was unstoppable. A man on a mission, he cut through Eddie Davis as if he weren't even there, knocking him out in Round Two. In the space of time it took to throw his fierce right hand, Donny became the light heavyweight champion of the world and a true hero to boot.

Donny reigned as champion until November 1988, when he lost his belt to a legend, Sugar Ray Leonard, in a big Las Vegas bout. Donny had Leonard in trouble early in the fight but couldn't put him away. Sugar Ray fought back ferociously to win and reclaim his championship title.

The Golden Boy lost his title belt, but in all the right ways Donny will be a champion for all time. He became what he needed most as a boy — a strong male role model, a hero.

Donny lives on Vancouver Island with his wife and two children, surrounded by love and affection. He still shines brightly as the Golden Boy, and he is a terrific father.

39

Larry Walker
Baseball

──∞∞∞──

Hometown: Maple Ridge, B.C.

IN 1887 JAMES "TIP" O'NEILL, THE PRIDE OF WOODSTOCK, Ontario, became one of baseball's biggest attractions when he led the big league in average and starred for the St. Louis Browns. O'Neill was the first Canadian to ever win baseball's coveted batting crown. One hundred and eleven years later Larry Walker, the pride of Maple Ridge, British Columbia, became the second.

Larry was only six years old when the legendary team of Canadian NHL players met the Soviet Union's great national team in 1972. After Canada pulled out the victory in the last minute, Larry joined his family, who were gathered around the TV set, and almost everybody else in the country in wild celebration. Larry loved hockey — he still does. As a boy he grew up with a stick in his hand and, like the rest of his pals, Walker wanted to play Canada's game at the highest level possible — the National Hockey League.

Larry was a gifted athlete and a tough hockey player who fought his way up to the junior level and played with Cam Neely. Neely went on to a solid NHL career. Larry took a different, less Canadian course.

In the off-season Larry played baseball to keep his competitive juices flowing and he played fastball for his dad's team. Along with his three older brothers, Walker helped turn the squad into a provincial powerhouse. Larry could crush the ball and he played defence like he was born for the job. At 16 he was named the Most Valuable Player in the league. He was a shy kid then and was a bit embarrassed to accept the trophy at the banquet dinner in front of a roomful of men, but at that point the ballpark was all about having fun. At the arena, things were far more serious for young Larry Walker, MVP.

In 1984 Larry was in his 18th year and a graduate of Maple Ridge Senior High School. Decisions about his future loomed. A letter from the Montreal Expos arrived just before his birthday and clarified everything. A local Montreal scout had enough faith in Walker to talk the team into giving the Canadian kid a shot. The Expos wanted to sign Larry to a contract as an undrafted amateur free agent. They wanted him to report to their Florida complex at West Palm Beach.

Larry could have played hockey at the tier-two junior level for another season had he chosen that route. But green grass, lawn sprinklers and baseball offered a nice alternative. As well, it was the Montreal Expos and Montreal, like Larry, loved hockey. The future was looking clearer for young Larry.

Larry stored his hockey bag and sticks in the garage; he packed his cleats and gloves and some clothes and then drove his pickup truck clear across the continent from British Columbia to Florida. He was heading south to see if he could become a baseball player for the Montreal Expos. It wasn't hockey, but it was definitely Canadian.

Larry's natural talent and aptitude for the game were remarkable. He ate up the distance between his knowledge of the sport and that of his American teammates who came to camp better schooled in the finer baseball arts. But Larry could out-hit and out-hustle all of them. He was just happy to be there and it showed.

Within two seasons, Baseball America selected Larry as a Class A All-Star. The next year he became a member of the 1987 Southern League AA All-Stars. Management was happy. A homegrown baseball player was moving up fast.

In the winter of 1988 Larry went south to play winter ball in Mexico. On a rain-soaked field he tore up his right knee so badly that he had to sit out the entire 1988 season. Larry studied the game from the sidelines and came back in 1989 to become an AAA American Association All-Star. The Expos called him up to the Major Leagues that fall and he appeared in 20 games for Montreal. Larry was a big league baseball player from that moment on.

In the 1992 season Larry broke through to the upper level of the game. He represented the Expos at the All-Star Game; he won a Rawlings Gold Glove Award and a Silver Slugger Award. He added another Gold Glove honour in 1993. In 1994 he missed a third of the season with a torn rotator cuff in his right (throwing) shoulder, but he returned to play first base and keep his bat in the lineup through the pennant race. He did not want to sit on the bench. The big crowds at Olympic Stadium loved Larry's "hockey" attitude and his passion.

Expo fans were devastated at the end of that season when a labour dispute cancelled the post-season and they saw their World Series dream turn into an arbitration night-mare. The owners dug in on one side; the players dug in on the other. For the first time since 1905 there would be no

World Series and the Expos had a team that was poised to win it all. Uncertainty over the future turned to panic and management dismantled the team. Montreal fans have never come back to the strength of the 1994 season.

Larry signed as free agent with the Colorado Rockies in 1995. By then he was one of the most sought-after and gifted all-round players in the game. In 1996 he broke his collarbone by slamming into the fence at Colorado while chasing down a fly. The fans loved his desire. He went all out all the time and the surgeries just kept coming.

In 1997 Larry made history and became the first Canadian to be named Most Valuable Player in the Major Leagues. The following year he led all players in batting average and joined Tip O'Neill in the Canadian Club as Major League batting champion. He won that crown again in 1999 and then again for a third time in 2001. The third crown put him in the company of baseball's greatest legends.

Throughout his career Larry played every defensive position except shortstop. His hitting heroics have been equally matched by seven Gold Glove Awards for defensive excellence. These are Hall of Fame statistics.

Larry has played through injuries that would end many careers. He has played in pain in nearly every game since his knee injury in Mexico. He has said that he plays harder than the rest because that's what he was taught to do as a young boy at the hockey rink.

40

Caroline Brunet
Sprint kayak

Hometown: Lac Beauport, Quebec

CAROLINE BRUNET COMES FROM AN AREA THAT HAS produced some of Canada's finest athletes. Lac Beauport, Quebec, has given us national and world alpine skiers, cross-country skiers, cyclists and moguls skiers. This region is considered to be the birthplace of aerials skiing — headquarters to the vaunted Quebec Air Force. It's a very beautiful place.

In her childhood Caroline took a different path. She picked up the double-bladed paddle, slipped into a kayak and spent countless hours on the lake. She grew stronger and gained confidence in the craft. Then she started to race her friends and win. After that, she got faster every season.

In her 13th summer Caroline entered her first real race at the 1982 Lac Beauport Canoe and Kayak Club's annual regatta — she won going away. From that point on, Caroline kept winning, which was good because she really hated losing so much. By her own admission, it was never the winning that drove her but rather the fear of losing.

Caroline's instinct to be first to the finish line propelled her onto the national team within five years. In 1988 — at 19 — she qualified for Canada's Olympic team and made the journey to Seoul. At the same time as she worked on her sport and conditioning, she also worked at becoming bilingual. She was reaching her goals one stroke at a time.

In Seoul Caroline didn't get into the finals of the K-1 500-metre race. She finished 13th overall. She hated that. Four years later in Barcelona, she moved up to seventh place. She hated that too and decided to radically change her training program and her life.

Caroline packed up and moved her training centre to Denmark. In Europe she'd face the best. And being the best is what she was most interested in.

Brunet took Christian Frederiksen as her coach. A former world champion, he'd already been to the highest step on the podium. The very place Caroline aimed for.

She spent more and more time on the water paddling — more than 30 hours per week. She also spent another dozen or so hours in the gym. Because her sport has a low profile she had to spend a lot of time trying to get enough sponsorship money to help pay for her coach, her equipment, her rent and her groceries.

In 1993 at the World Championships in Copenhagen Caroline finished third in the K-1. She was 24 and had finally reached the podium. A year later, in Mexico, she placed fourth in the 500-metre K-1 and third in the 200-metre solo race at the same meet in Mexico City. In 1995 she took second place at both distances in Duisburg, Germany. Caroline was right on course for a shot at Olympic glory in Atlanta in 1996.

When Caroline won the silver medal in Georgia, she was content — for a while. But the more she replayed the race on videotape and in her mind, the more it ate at her. The margin between gold and silver was .02 seconds. She vowed to erase the gap. Caroline Brunet started her streak at home in 1997.

The World Kayak Championships were held in Dartmouth, Nova Scotia, and Caroline ignited the crowd with three first-place finishes. She won the 200-, 500- and 1000-metre K-1 races to dominate the solo events. One year later in Hungary, she defended her K-1 200- and 500-metre titles and placed second in the K-1 1000-metre race. In 1999, she swept all three titles again at Milan. Then she teamed up with Karen Furneaux of Waverly, Nova Scotia, to finish second in the 500-metre K-2 contest.

The 1999 season established Caroline as the best paddler in the world. She won the Lou Marsh Trophy and Canada's Outstanding Athlete of the Year and accepted the award graciously. But her gaze was already fixed on Sydney, Australia, and the 2000 Summer Olympics. She would be heavily favoured to win gold.

Caroline was honed to as fine an edge as an athlete can attain in Australia. She arrived a few months before the Games to train and acclimatize. There would only be two events in Sydney: the K-1 500-metre race and the K-2 over the same distance. Her partner in K-2 would be Furneaux.

On September 15 Caroline proudly carried Canada's flag into the dazzling opening ceremony at Sydney Olympic Stadium. Our team fell in behind her. Then on September 27 she won her K-1 heat and finished third with Karen in the K-2 to get into the finals of both races. Then she sat and waited.

The winds descended on the rowing course with Down-Under fury. The finals of canoe, kayak and rowing were all affected. Each day the athletes showed up and each day officials closed the course. On October 1, the final day of competition in Sydney, they decided to race. Caroline, with all her skill and might, was unable to overcome nature and on a windy course she placed second in the K-1 and fifth in the K-2 with her partner. Her second consecutive silver medal did not quench the fire.

In 2001 Caroline turned 32. To reach her dream of winning Olympic gold she'd have to dedicate another four years of her life to the quest. She took some time and decided to do that very thing. With a new coach, Frédéric Jobin, beside her, she came back in 2002 to take second in both the K-1 200- and 500-metre sprints and place fifth in the 1000-metre race in Sevilla, Spain. In 2003 she served notice that she was all the way back when she won the 200 K-1 and finished second in the 500.

Caroline's desire to win Olympic gold has seen her fight to the very top of the kayak world and to stay there for nearly a decade. At 35, she will compete in her fifth Olympic Games in Athens in August 2004.

41

Daniel Igali
Wrestling

Hometown: Burnaby, B.C.

THE OLYMPIC CHAMPION IN THE 69-KILOGRAM FREESTYLE wrestling class was born in Nigeria in 1974. His full name is Baraledei Daniel Igali. His people, the Ijaw tribe, are accomplished wrestlers and Daniel grew up in a family of 21 children, amid plenty of partners to grapple with.

In the Ijaw style of wrestling, the match is over as soon as one opponent is taken to the ground — no matter how. As a boy, Daniel spent the days wrestling in his village of Eniwari, the way a Canadian kid would play hockey. Like any gifted athlete, his skill grew as the days passed. Soon Daniel was winning most of his matches even against the heavier boys. He was quick and decisive when he moved in for the throw.

In 1990 when Daniel was 16 he went to his first freestyle-wrestling tournament — the senior wrestling National Senior Tournament of Nigeria. He surprised everyone except himself when he won his division. His village celebrated.

Daniel was excited. The victory meant that he could travel to neighbouring countries as a member of Nigeria's wrestling team. The economic and political uncertainty in his country made him happy to be outside its borders. He saw how other people lived. He learned that it was good to hope and okay to dream.

In 1993 Daniel travelled to the African Wrestling Championships in Pretoria, South Africa. Every part of the trip thrilled the young athlete: packing, meeting his team and especially flying. A year later he flew north to Cairo, Egypt, and won the Continental title in his class. Baraledei Daniel Igali of Eniwari, Nigeria, was a 1994 Champion of All Africa. He was welcomed home to his village as a conquering hero.

In 1994 Daniel packed for the trip of his young life. He was flying all the way to Canada — to Victoria, British Columbia, for the Commonwealth Games. He kissed his family goodbye and left to meet his destiny. Daniel's 11th-place finish in Victoria is a sidebar to the real story: he left his team and defected to the host country, Canada. He knew that he'd have to leave his home and family behind in order to reach for his destiny.

Daniel became a student at Simon Fraser University and went to work with coaches Dave McKay and Mike Jones. They refined his raw talent and Igali worked hard. Then he proceeded to run off 116 straight victories for the Simon Fraser wrestling team in his three years at the school. McKay and Jones had set him on the course to gold.

By 1998 Daniel was a proud member of Canada's national wrestling team. At the World Championships in Tehran, Iran, that year, he finished fourth and gave Canada a strong presence at the meet. He followed that up with a second-place finish at the World Cup.

In 1999 Daniel travelled to Ankara, Turkey, and won the World Championship tournament. The experience made him feel like a king.

Five days after winning the world title, Daniel received devastating news. His Canadian host, who had been battling cancer, was dead. The young wrestler mourned the passing of Maureen Matheny, who'd become his Canadian mother figure. He carried her memory and fierce pride in his heart to Australia in 2000.

At the Sydney Olympics Daniel fought off every move and countered every attack to win six straight tough matches and become the Olympic gold-medal champion. When he unfurled his Canadian flag, he said later that the first person he thought about was Maureen Matheny.

When Daniel received his gold medal and stood to salute our flag and anthem, he cried. Many Canadians cried with him. Tears of joy happen that way sometimes.

Daniel came home to Athlete of the Year honours. His journey touched many hearts. After the accolades and celebrations were over, he raised enough money to return to Nigeria and build a permanent water pump in his home village. The people there welcomed their Olympic champion with love and affection. And, in 2001, he fulfilled another lifelong dream when he graduated from Simon Fraser University with a degree in Criminology.

Now when someone turns on the tap in Eniwari, Nigeria, they think of a great Canadian, Daniel Igali.

42

Clara Hughes
Cycling and long-track speed skating

Hometown: Winnipeg

CLARA HUGHES WAS BORN ON SEPTEMBER 27, 1972 — ONE day before Paul Henderson scored for Canada to beat the Soviet Union National Hockey Team in Moscow. She spent the first few days of her life breathing pure Canadian pride. So her patriotism is easy to understand. She has a maple leaf on her soul.

At 15 Clara, like the rest of her fellow Canadians, sat glued to the television set from the 13th to the 28th of February, 1988, watching the Calgary Winter Olympic Games: watching the great Gaetan Boucher in his final skate; watching Bonnie Blair of the USA and Yvonne van Gennip of the Netherlands win gold at the beautiful new speed-skating oval. Right in the middle of the spectacle she fell in love with the sport. Clara Hughes announced to her mom and dad that she wanted to win a medal for Canada at the Olympic Games in speed skating more than anything in the world.

Mr. and Mrs. Hughes supported Clara's interest completely, even though the sporting world was unfamiliar to Clara's artistic family. Her lack of motivation had been holding her back academically. Anything that would turn her around would be explored. So Clara set off to speed-skating summer camp with a set of hockey skates and an Olympic-sized dream.

The following winter in 1989 Clara went to skate with long-time Winnipeg coach Peter Williamson. At the Canadian Junior Championships, she took second place in the 1500-metre mass-start event. She was selected Manitoba Junior Athlete of the Year. Her marks were improving too. The Hughes household was a happy one.

The discipline Clara needed to skate well became woven into her life. She was growing and balanced. But in Clara's second season, coach Williamson left Winnipeg to move to the new Olympic indoor oval facility in Calgary and most of the senior skaters went with him. Clara felt lost.

But then fate stepped in to lend a positive hand. Clara heard through a friend that the Manitoba Cycling Association had an empty spot on the provincial team for the upcoming Western Canada Games. She tried out and fell into the sport like a natural. She stepped up to the national team almost immediately.

Cycling wasn't speed skating, but winning felt good no matter what the sport. Clara didn't feel so lost anymore. She'd found a new outlet. With her long red hair and her Canadian team uniform, she became one of the most identifiable racers on the course.

Clara started out racing on the track, but then she switched to the road race and wore Canada's cycling jersey for 10 years. Hughes represented Canada at three Pan Am Games, three Commonwealth Games and two Olympic Games. In all, Clara held 18 national titles as a cyclist.

The whole time Clara was building up her impressive cycling résumé she stayed in touch with speed skating. In 1992 in Calgary she won both the 3000- and 5000-metre races at the Canadian Junior Championships after being away from the ice for three seasons. She entered the event because she happened to be in Calgary at the time, training for cycling. Clara just couldn't shake her love of speed skating.

In her Olympic dream, Clara's medal always came in speed skating. So she was a bit surprised in Atlanta at the 1996 Summer Games when she won Olympic bronze in the cycling individual time trial. She was completely blown away a few days later when she repeated in the road race. The two Olympic bronze medals made her one of Canada's Atlanta heroes.

In the years after Atlanta, Clara suffered through a series of painful injuries and at one point slipped into retirement. But the allure of representing Canada drew her back to her bike and she went to Sydney in 2000 as a member of Canada's Olympic team. At the conclusion of the Olympics she decided to hang up her bike and to follow her heart. Clara had to return to the ice.

At the Olympic speed-skating team trials just one year after Sydney, Clara Hughes posted the fourth fastest time in the history of the 5000-metre race. Her years as a cyclist only helped her as a skater. She was strong and smooth and tireless.

At the Olympic Winter Games in Salt Lake City she qualified 10th out of 32 finalists and then flew to a bronze medal, finishing one place ahead of her teammate and fellow Winnipegger Cindy Klaussen.

Clara was the first Canadian to ever win medals at both the Winter and the Summer Olympics and one of only four world athletes to accomplish the feat. Her Olympic dream at last came to pass at the medal ceremony in Utah. She had won a medal for Canada in speed skating at the Winter Olympics.

In the summer of 2002, Clara started to ride again and, at 30 years old, won gold and bronze medals in cycling at the Commonwealth Games in Manchester, England. Then in 2003 she went to the Pan American Games in the Dominican Republic and took first-, second- and third-place finishes in her three races. Between these competitions, Clara also became the first Canadian since 1972 to win an individual event (the 5000-metre) at the World All-Round Speed Skating Championships in Sweden. Then she became the first non-European to win a 3000-metre World Cup race. She finished the 2002/03 World Cup season second overall in the 3000- and 5000-metre distances. She closed that season with a second-place finish in the 5000-metre at the World Single Distance Speed Skating Championships.

After that dominant season, Clara was forced to make yet another choice: concentrate on cycling and Athens in the summer of 2004 or continue speed skating and focus on 2006 in Italy. Clara chose to follow the dream and to skate on. In March 2004 in Seoul she won the 5000-metre race at the World Single Distance Championships. Her Olympic gold-medal dream still shines.

Just as Paul Henderson did on the day after she was born, Clara Hughes has also scored for Canada.

43

Donovan Bailey
Sprinter

DONOVAN BAILEY DIDN'T PAY MUCH ATTENTION TO PURE running when he was a kid growing up in Manchester, Jamaica. He liked school okay. He got good marks and played soccer, cricket and basketball and played them all well, but lining up and racing just didn't appeal to him — at least not yet it didn't.

When Donovan was 13, his mom and dad immigrated to Canada and settled with their five children in Oakville. Donovan went to Queen Mary Park High School, where he did very well academically and tore up the basketball court. When he graduated, Donovan decided to go to Sheridan College to study and play for that school's varsity basketball team. He was the fastest player on the team. Actually, he was the fastest player in the league, but Sheridan didn't have a track team and in spite of the urging of friends, Donovan never seriously sought out a coach.

After college, Donovan became a stockbroker and did very well at the job. He liked Bay Street, liked the rush of doing business, but he needed something more intense to feed his considerable competitive nature. And so in 1990, when Donovan was already 23, he decided to dabble in track.

He went to work out that year with coach Erwin Turney, but Bailey wasn't very dedicated and his best time of the year, 10.42 seconds, reflected this attitude. Good but not spectacular. The lacklustre time bore no resemblance whatsoever to Donovan's true potential. He was built for speed.

In 1994 Donovan met legendary sprint-coach Dan Pfaff. One of Dan's former students at Louisiana State University was Glenroy Gilbert, a member of Canada's 1993 world championship second-place 4 × 100-metre relay team, along with Bruny Surin of Montreal and Robert Esmie of Sudbury. The sprinters were all impressed with Donovan's natural speed and they pushed him to take the sport more seriously. Once he threw himself into training in 1994, his personal best for the season dropped to 10.03. That's rapid transit.

In 1995 at his first World Championships in Gothenburg, Sweden, Donovan, a virtual unknown at this elite level, won the 100-metre race in 9.97 seconds. His fellow Canadian, Bruny Surin, came second and they joined Esmie and Gilbert to win the 4 × 100-metre relay for Canada. It was the surprise of the season. Donovan was also awarded the Lou Marsh Trophy that year.

Canadian fans held their collective breath through the heats at the Atlanta Olympic Games on July 27, 1996. Our national track team was still hurting and embarrassed by the Ben Johnson steroid scandal eight years earlier in Seoul. But Donovan was confident the whole way through. He'd race for pride, for gold and for the redemption of his country on Saturday night in Georgia.

The stadium was packed. In the heart of the New South there was no mistaking who the crowd favourites were. Dennis Mitchell, Mike Marsh and Michael Green would all line up at the start for the USA. When the sprinters made their entrance, the excitement built like steam in the Olympic Stadium.

The drama only intensified in the starters' area as each sprinter stepped into the blocks to get ready. The top nearly blew off the place when defending Olympic champion Linford Christie of Great Britain made his second false start; Ato Boldon had made one too. The officials disqualified Christie, but he wouldn't leave the field quickly and had to be escorted off the track. The pressure in the building reached a climax.

Then the runners got off cleanly and Donovan overhauled the field just past the halfway point. A wall of flashbulbs followed alongside him down the straightaway. He hit the finish line in a state of euphoria — flushed with the rapture of victory. The gold was Donovan's — so was the new world record of 9.84 seconds. Frankie Fredericks of Namibia took the silver in 9.89 and Ato Boldon of Trinidad won bronze with a time of 9.90. The Americans were shut out of the medals.

Donovan stood in the pure light of Olympic glory, draped in Canada's flag, in front of thousands in the Olympic Stadium. Fans across Canada and all over Jamaica celebrated. The memory of Ben Johnson's horrible scandal dissolved into the Atlanta night. Somehow, old wounds healed that night.

One week later Donovan ran the anchor leg in the 4 x 100-metre relay and with Robert Esmie, Glenroy Gilbert and Bruny Surin won Canada's second track gold in Atlanta. The country stood proudly as the Red Leaf flew the highest at the medal presentation for the second time in Atlanta.

At the World Championships in 1997 Donovan placed second in the 100-metre race and anchored the relay team to a defence of their world title. It would be the final great day for this relay team that became a dynasty. A year later, Donovan tore his Achilles tendon and sat out most of the season. The injury forced him to miss the 1999 season as well.

While preparing for the Sydney Olympics in 2000, Donovan tore his hamstring at a meet in Stockholm. He worked harder than ever to recuperate properly and build back his strength so that he could defend his Olympic championship in Australia. However, while training in Brisbane just before the Games, Donovan came down with a flu bug that swept through Canada's training facility and the Olympic Village. He tried to compete and was able to make it through his first heat. But he was just too sick and he fell out of the race in a second-round heat.

On August 6, 2001, Donovan ran his last 100-metre sprint in front of a home crowd in Edmonton at the World Championships. Canada's greatest sprinter retired from the track.

Donovan has returned to the world of stock brokering. He also runs a sport management firm and co-owns a construction company, with one of his brothers. He travels often to Jamaica.

44

Silken Laumann
Rowing

Hometown: Mississauga

IN MIDSUMMER 1992 SILKEN LAUMANN WON AN OLYMPIC bronze medal in the single sculls rowing competition at Barcelona. Her unlikely journey to that podium in Spain was one of the most followed, one of the most difficult, and one of the most celebrated in the history of Canadian sports.

Silken's love of sports was there from the very beginning. Her dad played soccer in his youth back in Germany and her older sister, Danielle, was already a member of Canada's national rowing team by the time Silken got to high school.

As a girl, Silken fell in love with gymnastics while watching Nadia Comaneci of Romania win gold at the Montreal Olympics in 1976. A lot of girls did back in that summer. But Silken grew fast as a teenager and, at 5 feet 10 inches, she outgrew her childhood passion. Her focus switched to the track, and through high school she carved out a very good career as an 800-metre runner. But the pounding of running took a toll and injuries slowed her advance up the national ranking system. Then Danielle talked her into giving rowing a try. Silken slipped into that tippy little boat and never looked back.

After just a few months of hard training, Silken joined Danielle on the national team. She quickly established herself as a force and earned a spot in the quad sculls boat that won the U.S. Championship. In 1987 she captured gold at the Pan Am Games single sculls competition. A year later and just 20 years old, she lined up with her sister at the start of the Los Angeles Olympics double sculls final. The Laumann sisters thrilled Canada when they won a bronze medal that day. The future looked great, and our rowing team looked to be filled with promise.

Danielle retired after Los Angeles and Silken suffered from a pinched sciatic nerve condition that kept her from working at the pace she wanted. With the Seoul Olympics on the horizon, team officials decided to pair Silken with another excellent single sculls athlete, Kay Worthington, in the doubles event. The pair never found the chemistry needed to get to the Olympic podium. None of the other Canadian boats did either. The promise of L.A. was unresolved, the whole experiment looked upon as a failure. The rowing program would have to regroup. So would Silken.

Silken turned her back on pairs and re-dedicated herself to single sculls. In 1990 she went to the World Championships and won a silver medal. Then she moved her training base west to Victoria, where she could work with coach Mike Sprachlan of the men's team. They found the right chemistry between athlete and coach, and Silken rose to the very top when in 1991 she burst into the lead and then beat back everybody's challenge at the World Championships.

The win helped re-establish Canada as a world rowing power and Silken went home to be recognized with the Lou Marsh Trophy as Canada's Athlete of the Year. With the

Summer Olympics of Barcelona just around the corner, Silken stood alone as the most dominant rower on the face of the planet.

For 1992, the Olympic year, coach Sprachlan and Silken laid out a plan that was singularly focused on the Barcelona regatta. The Games opened on July 25. Their mission was clear — capture Spanish gold. Silken was locked on the target and unbeatable in the early season. By May she was racing in Europe, and on the morning of May 15th, while warming up on the training course at Essen, Germany, Silken's shell was accidentally broadsided by a men's double sculls boat travelling at high speed. The German boat ripped through Silken's shell and crushed her leg while ripping her flesh from the bone. The sports world was shocked.

Silken was in and out of surgery for nearly two weeks. Pins held her leg together. A series of grafting procedures was performed to remove tissue from her hips in order to give her leg new skin. She was in constant, throbbing pain. Her German doctors told the press that she'd be lucky to walk again, never mind row. Silken went home to Victoria to heal and contemplate her future.

Three weeks after the accident, Silken's husband, John Wallace, lovingly lowered her into a shell. John, a member of Canada's gold-medal heavy-eights crew in Los Angeles, knew that even though Barcelona was just five weeks away, Silken had to try and he had to help. She couldn't walk, but maybe she could row.

Silken started to stroke and then she fell into the rhythm of the oars. She could do it. She could row. She fought back the pain and together they did it again the next day and the next. She wasn't going to let anything stand in her way.

She was going to Spain. With the whole world watching, Silken managed not only to get to Barcelona, but also to claw her way through the heats and into the Olympic single sculls final. In an intense race, she fought with every gram of courage she had and won a bronze medal. Gold went to her long-time rival Elisabeth Lipa of Romania.

Silken won millions of hearts when she stood on the podium while Canada's flag was raised during the medal presentation. Her comeback defied all odds. Bronze was never more precious. There were tears in many Canadian eyes that day.

Silken rounded out her brilliant Olympic career in July 1996 on Lake Lanier in Georgia, where she won a silver medal for Canada in single sculls at the Atlanta Olympic Games. She retired after the 1996 season.

In 1999 Silken was inducted into the Canadian Sports Hall of Fame. Her time is now spent working for charities, being a mother, rowing and coaching young rowers.

45

Kathleen Heddle and Marnie McBean
Rowing

———⁂———

Hometowns: Vancouver, B.C., and London, Ontario

KATHLEEN HEDDLE AND MARNIE MCBEAN WEREN'T EVEN a team until 1991. But within five years of rowing together that first time, they became one of the best our country has ever seen.

Kathleen started to row for the University of British Columbia in 1985 by default. Her chosen sport was volleyball, but when her options on that team became limited, she switched to the varsity rowing program. She refocused her goals and left the wood floor behind for a new career on the water. At 19 Heddle took up one of the most demanding of all sports. From the start, she was a great team player — quiet, dependable and fearless.

Marnie went to the University of Western Ontario, more than halfway across the country in London. She rowed single sculls and loved the solitary game. She worked tirelessly and constantly to improve and started to move up through the national rankings. From the start, she was loud, strong and fearless.

Kathleen became a national team member in 1987 and Marnie moved up in 1989. Two years later, they were put together in the coxless pairs shell for the first time as an experiment. They were complete opposites and the chemistry worked right away. They beat the defending world champions their first time out together. Then, to prove it was no fluke they won the 1991 World Coxless Pairs Championship. At the same regatta, they both stepped into the Canadian eights boat and helped win that event too. The experiment had clearly been an overwhelming success.

Marnie and Kathleen were opposites as personalities but they both thrived on hard work. They had to. Rowers work every day on the water for hours. Each stroke must be perfect; the rhythm, perfect; the unison, perfect. Each movement in the boat has to be perfect.

After three or four hours rowing they had to do dryland training in the gym for another two or three hours. But they did it together — put in the hours — pushed each other onward. Upward too.

In 1992 the biggest rowing story at the Barcelona Olympic Games centred on Silken Laumann's quest. Millions worldwide watched her improbable comeback from a freak injury to her leg to win a bronze medal in the single sculls event. It was an extraordinary achievement.

Behind the headlines another great Canadian story played out in Barcelona. Kathleen and Marnie dominated their event, winning coxless pairs gold for Canada. Then, just like at the worlds, they stepped into the eights boat and helped power another Canadian boat to gold-medal honours. Kathleen and Marnie became the golden girls of the rowing world in Barcelona in relative obscurity.

After returning home from Spain and accepting the accolades of Canadian fans, Kathleen called it a career. She headed home to Vancouver to settle down and start a new life.

Marnie wasn't through, though, and returned to her first rowing love, the single sculls in Silken Laumann's injury-driven absence. She performed well on the 1993 World Cup circuit, winning a silver medal at the World Championships in Roundnice, Czechoslovakia, and might have continued in the solo boat, but when Silken returned Marnie was forced to come up with a whole new plan.

Marnie began to talk to Kathleen about coming out of retirement for the Atlanta Olympic Games in 1996. Kathleen finally agreed. Together they went to the 1995 World Championships in Tampere, Finland, where they won the pairs title again and helped the quad team to a silver medal. Canada's boat was back.

At Lake Lanier in Georgia in July of 1996, Kathleen and Marnie rowed hard to catch up to Olympic glory. They cruised through the heats and into the final in fine form. Millions of Canadians tuned in to watch their race. When the race came down to the end, fans reached with the Canadians as they dug deep inside to pull each other through.

The final 10 strokes of the race saw both the Chinese and Netherlands boats charging hard. Kathleen never faltered — she just kept rowing. Marnie was still leaning into her oars after they crossed the finish line. They performed like a perfect team and they were fearless that day. They defended their Olympic title and their gold medals made them the most-decorated Canadian Olympians of all time — something they accomplished together.

A few days later Kathleen and Marnie both stepped up to a bigger boat — this time the quads — and helped Canada's crew to a bronze-medal win. It was the perfect ending to their Olympic journey.

Kathleen retired after Atlanta — this time for good. Marnie stayed on to row sculls for Canada, winning a silver in the quad and a bronze in the eight at Munich, but a recurrent back injury forced her to retire just before the Sydney Olympics in 2000.

Kathleen Heddle and Marnie McBean captured three Olympic gold medals and a bronze. Marnie is the only woman in the world to have a top-three placing in six different heavyweight boats at world and Olympic competitions.

46

Lori Kane
Golf

Hometown: Charlottetown

LORI KANE GREW UP ON PRINCE EDWARD ISLAND. WITH its rolling hills, lush grass and ocean breezes there is no more perfect place on Earth to set a golf course than PEI.

When Lori was five years old her dad, Jack, taught her how to swing a golf club. He loved the game and was building his career as a golf course manager. He also had strong views on how to teach the game to kids. His approach was simple and he was very patient with Lori. He showed her an appreciation for the relaxing nature of golf; he stressed fun and accomplishment and, above all, there was no yelling. Lori's talent bloomed in the nurturing environment.

In high school Lori played most team sports but loved basketball over the rest. Her coach Dave MacNeil recognized Lori's superior athletic talent and started to help her work on her mental game especially for the solitary sport that best suited her talents. She responded and started winning golf tournaments.

Throughout her career as a professional Lori has constantly returned to her Island roots for support and balance. She's given her dad and MacNeil a great deal of the credit for her success. At home she's just Lori from Charlottetown

— and happy to be just another member at the Belvedere Golf and Country Club, even though she's the best golfer they've ever seen.

After high school Lori went to Acadia University in Wolfville, Nova Scotia. She kept her game up and by 1989 was one of the top juniors in the country. She represented Canada at a number of international junior tournaments and in 1991 she played on the commonwealth team and then turned around and won the Mexican Amateur Championships. The next year she moved up to the Canadian World Amateur team and travelled to New Zealand. Just Lori from Charlottetown was seeing the world and golf was her ticket.

Kane was running out of golf options at home so she set her sights on the Ladies Professional Golf Association (LPGA) tour and the big-time pro tour. If she could make it there she could earn a living doing exactly what she loved most — travelling the world and golfing.

In 1996 Lori made her debut on the big-money LPGA tour at the PING/Welch's Championships in Boston, where she tied for eighth place. Her goal for the 1997 season was simple: Gain some experience and get better — lower the scores one week at a time. She didn't focus on winning, but rather on playing well. She had a great season and finished second four times. Twice she went into sudden-death playoffs at big tournaments. She wound up 11th on the money list and by all accounts had arrived as a player to watch on the tour. Her supporters back in Kane-country PEI were ecstatic.

Through the 1998 and 1999 seasons Lori became one of the most dependable golfers on the tour. She put in more under-par rounds than any other golfer in both those years.

She played constantly and lowered her scores just as she wanted. In 1999 she was one of the top-five money-earners in the game and even scored a rare tournament hole in one. On most weekends her name was on the leaderboard right up until the very end. She was always close but never in the winner's circle and she had to know why.

Midway through the 2000 season Lori went back to the Island to find her centre. She talked to the people she most trusted in the game and in life — her dad, her high school coach Dave MacNeil, friends and family. When Lori's caddy Danny Sharp suggested she tweak her goals slightly, a light went on. Lori had been focused on the components of the game instead of the whole package. She worried about each shot rather than about winning the tournament. She had lowered her scores, improved her swing and stayed at the top, but she had not moved over to the winner's side. Lori had become the best player in the world without a tour victory. Her nine second-place finishes gave little comfort. Once she figured all that out, Kane got hungry.

Lori went back to the tour and in early August won her first LPGA championship at the Michelob Light Classic in St. Louis. The ice had at last been broken. Then the Canadian star went on a tear and won the New Albany Golf Classic and the Mizuno Open before the 2000 season ended. She finished the year in fifth place on the money list with nearly $1 million in winnings. She came home to a family celebration and was named winner of the Bobbie Rosenfeld Canadian Female Athlete of the Year award by the Canadian sports media.

Lori Kane is one of the top professional golfers in the world. She is a fan favourite wherever she plays; she's well respected by her rivals and she's a hero to aspiring young golfers everywhere. Lori keeps a home in Florida during the season and spends as much time as possible in PEI every year. She has become a proud spokesperson for that province's growing golf industry.

47

Simon Whitfield
Triathlon

Hometown: Kingston, Ontario

WHEN SIMON WHITFIELD BROUGHT HOME AN academically disappointing report card from high school in Kingston, his parents called a family meeting. Although Simon's performance in sports was excellent, his performance in class was suffering. The Whitfields decided to send Simon to his dad's old school — in Sydney, Australia.

Simon did well in Australia — his friends dubbed him "Happy" because of his zest for life. His marks improved, he learned how to set goals and then reach them and he discovered a sport that he loved — triathlon. He loved the stamina sports, and the combination of distance swimming and a cycling road race followed by a long run suited him just fine. Triathlon satisfied his passion for a healthy lifestyle and fuelled his competitive drive. As well, he was really good at the marathon segment of the race and loved to close in on the leaders from behind.

By the time he came back to Canada, Simon was dedicated to the sport. He split his time between Australia and Victoria so he could train all year long. In 1995 Simon became the Canadian Junior Triathlon Champion and a member of the national team. His mom and dad couldn't have been prouder. So they thought, at the time anyway.

In 1997 Simon headed back to Australia for the World Triathlon Championship at Perth. He broke into the top 10 with a ninth-place finish and then came home to become the 1998 Canadian Triathlon Champion. In 1999 Simon defended his national title successfully, placed seventh at the World Championships in Montreal, won a bronze medal at the Pan Am Games in Winnipeg and was named Canadian Triathlete of the Year. It was a very good season.

With Sydney and the 2000 Olympics circled on his calendar, Simon began to pick up his training. For the first time in history, triathlon would be a full Olympic-medal sport. The gold medal had the added weight of history. For Simon it would be just like competing at home.

Because Simon's knowledge of Sydney was so solid — his grandmother lived close to part of the marathon course — he set out a route in Victoria that was similar. Throughout the year he swam, ran and cycled at Thetis Lake and Rocky Point Road. In his mind, he was already in Sydney hauling in the medals. In competition Simon proved time after time that he could run better than most. As he ran, he pre-played the scene he envisioned for Sydney — glory in the shadow of the Opera House.

Simon laid out his plan for Sydney and then executed it to perfection. In the lead-up to Australia, he placed second at a World Cup International Triathlon Union (ITU) race in Corner Brook, Newfoundland, second at another in Rio de Janeiro in Brazil and fourth at the World Cup ITU competition in Toronto.

Simon competed often to stay in top shape and enjoyed the rivalries building on the tour. Many of his opponents on race day were also his friends. Camaraderie among triathletes runs high. They have to fight through so much together that respect comes easy.

When Canada's Olympic team arrived in Sydney, Simon was right at home. Race day was Thursday, September 17. High winds from earlier in the week that had cancelled sailing events were calm now and the sun was shining on Sydney Harbour. Simon was the only Canadian competitor in the race. Week One was drawing to a close and Canada did not yet have a gold medal. Simon could see all that changing in his mind.

Simon came through the swim stage in good shape. A new suit that arrived just before the start fit well, kept him warm and made him comfortable out on the swim course. Many of his Australian friends showed up with their faces painted half-green for Australia and half-red for Canada. Red Leaf flags dotted the course and Simon settled in with a group of 15 riders through the cycling stage.

On the final lap of the road-race course one of the group leaders skidded-out at a narrow part of the track. Riders were crashing all around, but Simon got a foot down and stayed in the saddle of his bike. He got through the melee and pumped hard to get to the transition station. He shed his cycling gear, pulled on his running shoes, hydrated and ran onto the marathon course. His best was just ahead.

Simon grew stronger through the run as always. With the Australian athlete falling out of contention, Simon became the sentimental favourite as the crowd lined the course. When he ran past the Sydney Opera House, two countries cheered him on. The finish was in reach when Simon passed Jan Rehula of the Czech Republic and moved into second place. With 200 metres to go, German Stephan Vuckovic, the leader and a friend of Simon's, turned around just in time to see Simon sail past and into the lead. It was all over. The first-ever gold medal in Olympic triathlon was going to a Canadian. Simon Whitfield bathed in the cheers of the Sydney fans as he crossed the finish line.

IOC Vice-President Dick Pound awarded the gold medal to Simon at the presentation ceremony. From Montreal, Pound swam for Canada in Rome in 1960 and understood how hard it is to reach the Olympic podium. Both men fully enjoyed the playing of Canada's national anthem.

Simon continues to compete and is one of the world's top-ranked triathletes. He thrilled the Edmonton crowd with a gold-medal performance at the 2002 Commonwealth Games in Manchester, England. His parents have forgiven him for the bad report card.

48

Atlanta 4 × 100 Relay Team

1996 Olympics

THE DAY AFTER OAKVILLE'S DONOVAN BAILEY WON HIS 100-metre sprint gold medal in world record time at the Atlanta Olympics in 1996 he had to get up and head out to the practice field. There was much work still to be done. The 4 × 100-metre relay was just six days away on Saturday night at Olympic Stadium.

Donovan would run the anchor leg and knew he had to make the transition from being an inwardly focused athlete — sprinters must be concerned only for themselves — to becoming a team player and a leader.

The other members of Canada's relay team had to go through the same transition: Bruny Surin of Montreal, Glenroy Gilbert from Ottawa, Sudbury's Robert Esmie and Carlton Chambers of Mississauga knew they faced a formidable task. They had to get through the heats and into the Olympic final where the USA, running at home, would be the overwhelming crowd favourite. Surin, Gilbert and Esmie had been running together at major events since 1992; they knew the stadium would be an Olympic pressure cooker on that Saturday night in Georgia.

Canada's relay team was the reigning world champion, but the USA had never lost a 4 × 100-metre relay in the history of the Olympic Games (although they were disqualified once). Running against the U.S. team at home on the historic hundredth anniversary of the Olympics would be the biggest challenge the Canadian athletes had ever faced. American pride would be running high — that in itself was enough to bring Canada's team together.

In the heats, the athletes, along with coach Andy McInnis, elected to lead off with Carlton Chambers. The rest of the lineup had Glenroy run the second leg and Bruny run the third leg, with world and Olympic champion Donovan Bailey left to bring it home. Things went as expected in the heats, although Bruny's pass to Donovan was less than perfect and this caused a few anxious moments. But the baton got to the finish line in Bailey's tightly clenched fist and everyone breathed easier. The Saturday-night showdown was set. It was Canada vs. the USA. The rest of the field was really there to watch history unfold.

Before the final, the team met and decided that Robert Esmie should run the first leg. Chambers came out of the final heat with a minor injury and it was best to play it safe and go with the healthy runner. Esmie prepared by shaving "Relay Blast Off" into his haircut.

Olympic Stadium was filled for the biggest relay event of the day. The atmosphere was electric; flags waved everywhere — in a swirling sea of red, white and blue. It was difficult to find a Red Maple Leaf in the house.

On the march out to the track, the Canadians moved calmly and spoke very little to one another — signs that they were confident and ready. The Americans, though, were charged by the energy of the crowd and got caught up in the rah-rah of the moment. They started to yell encouragement to one another, trying to pump their teammates up even higher. The USA team was expending a lot of energy and the race had yet to be run. The whole time, Canada's team was filling up on the power and strength of the moment.

When Esmie took his mark, he became a legend in his hometown — Sudbury, Ontario. The crowd's cheering faded down to nothing. The stadium stood silent until the starter called his instructions and fired the pistol to start the race. Esmie, true to his haircut, blasted off. He held his own and passed off to Gilbert, who took the race away from the Americans right there on the second leg. Gilbert ran the race of his life that night at precisely the perfect time. Then Surin buried the field on the final bend. He raised his arms in triumph as soon as Bailey secured the baton safely in his grasp for the fast trip to the finish line. Canada's time was 37:69 compared to the hometeam USA's time of 38:05, a stunning victory for our team.

The Canadian runners came together at the far end of the track and someone handed them a Canadian flag. They stood triumphant together, draped in red and white while flashbulbs lit the scene at Olympic Stadium on a hot Georgia Saturday night. And millions of Canadians stood together with them. It was the greatest track and field moment in the history of sport in our country.

Montrealer Dick Pound, IOC vice president, presented the five members of Canada's relay team with their gold medals. Pound, who had competed for Canada as a swimmer in Rome in 1960, described the playing of "O Canada" that night as one of the sweetest moments of his career.

The legendary Atlanta team defended their world title in Greece the following season. They ran together for two more years until Donovan Bailey tore his Achilles tendon in 1998. Their 1997 victory ended a period of sprint dominance for Canada on the world stage. That victory established the team as one of the greatest in sprint relay history.

Eric Gagné
Baseball

THE SUMMER OF 1971 WAS ONE OF THE MOST MEMORABLE ever for Canadian baseball fans. That season, Fergie Jenkins won the National League Cy Young Award as a starting pitcher for the Chicago Cubs. Jenkins was the first Canadian to ever win the honour that is handed out annually to the game's dominant pitcher. Thirty-two years later, in the summer of 2003, Eric Gagné of the Los Angeles Dodgers, wearing his trademark goggles, a grungy hat and with his scraggy beard flying, locked down 55 saves and joined Fergie's exclusive club of Canadian Cy Young Award winners.

Eric grew up just north of Montreal. He was a diehard Canadiens fan from birth and joined the street parade when his team won the Stanley Cup in 1986, the year he was 10. Eric's hero was Canadiens goalie Patrick Roy. In the big games Roy always came through.

Eric also loved the Expos and his favourite player was third baseman Tim Wallach. Third base is called the hot corner in baseball because the action there can get tough sometimes, what with base runners, line drives, throw-downs, bunts and all. Wallach played hardest when it mattered most. Eric was always attracted to the whole idea of pressure.

Eric played hockey in the winter and in the summer, like a lot of Canadian boys, he headed to the local diamond. He became a standout starter in the Quebec Leagues, which are among the best in the country. In 1994 and 1995 he was star on Canada's Youth Team pitching staff. In a call-up to the national team he was converted into a reliever because the squad was so deep in starters. That year, Canada had guys like Ryan Dempster of B.C. on the staff, so Eric embraced the new role and tried to fit in. He liked relief work because it suited his tough, commanding demeanour. Although he excelled at the game, baseball still wasn't Eric's focus — he breathed hockey.

On the ice, Eric was a big open-ice hitter who was never afraid to drop the gloves. His knuckles still bear the scars of junior league hockey fights. Eric's goggles are the result of a high stick that caused some retina damage to his eye. He played defence in front of José Théodore as a teenager and made a strong contribution to the École secondaire poly-vante Edouard-Monpetit team. His goalie pal went on to play for the beloved Canadiens. Eric, though, went in an entirely different direction after high school.

At graduation Eric was faced with three choices and one tough decision. He could go to the University of Vermont to play hockey; he could head to Oklahoma and play baseball at junior college; or he could sign with the Chicago White Sox, who picked him in the 30th round of the 1994 high school draft, and head to the Instructional League in Florida.

Eric chose education. He decided to head to Seminole State Junior College in Oklahoma. When he arrived, he spoke very little English but he worked hard, studied with a tutor, watched TV, joked around with the guys on the team and soon became fluent in English. He also learned how to pitch more efficiently and impressed the scouts with his fearless attitude and willingness to challenge hitters. After the next season, Eric signed as an amateur free agent with the Los Angeles Dodgers for $75,000. They figured him to be a starter.

In 1996 the 20-year-old fireballer from Mascouche was assigned to A ball for the Savannah Sand Gnats and was pitching well in the Georgia heat until an elbow injury ended his season. He was ordered not to touch a baseball for six months following off-season surgery, and he sat out the entire 1997 campaign.

During rehabilitation, Eric developed a devastating change-up. His arsenal of pitches was deeper now. He moved to Vero Beach in the Florida State League in 1998, and as his arm began to get stronger, so did his fastball. In 1999 as a starter in AA ball for the San Antonio Missions, Eric won 12 games and was named Dodger Minor League Pitcher of the Year. He was called up to the Majors on September 7 and tossed six scoreless innings against the Florida Marlins batting lineup. Eric was a big leaguer, no doubt about it, but at 22 he was about to learn how hard it is to stay at the top.

During spring training in 2000, Eric was pencilled in to be a Dodgers starter. But he lost control of his fastball and was hammered by big league batting. He was demoted to AAA and bounced back and forth between there and the majors until September, when he regained command of his stuff and closed the year well with three straight wins. Although far from a Cy Young performance, this was much better than his season start.

In 2001 Eric turned his season completely around by getting off to a solid start. He had a hot April, but by May he was having control problems again and the team shipped him back to the minors. Eric was not happy, but he never let that show. He stayed positive. He reported to AAA ball and vowed to get back to L.A. Eric worked harder than ever on his focus and on the tough mental aspects of the game.

In mid-July the Dodgers sent for Eric again, only this time they wanted him to work long relief from the bullpen. He finished the season with decent enough numbers and passed the character test for the team's management, who saw nothing but good things — especially when Eric had control of his mighty fastball.

At spring training in 2002 the pitching situation for the Dodgers was murky and how Eric fit into the picture was even murkier. The Dodgers loved Eric's hard-nosed attitude and his taste for tight situations. In the ninth inning of the fourth game of the season, manager Jim Tracy decided to see if Eric could take out the hated San Francisco Giants. He sent for the Canadian to protect a Dodger lead. Eric shut the Giants down to win a save and Tracy handed him the game ball. Eric had a new job as the Los Angeles Dodgers closing pitcher.

By June, Eric was the National League Pitcher of the Month. On July 1 he picked up his 30th save and was selected to play for the NL All-Star team later that month. He finished the season with a league-leading 52 saves and a 1.97 earned run average. In L.A. Eric was the man.

In 2003 the Dodgers asked Eric to convert a lead into a win and earn the save a total of 55 times. He was successful on each and every one. He struck out 137 batters in 82 1/3 innings, an amount equalling 55 percent of the batters he faced, and setting Major League records. He had a 1.20 earned run average and dominated every statistical category.

To honour his unprecedented achievement, Eric was named Rolaids Relief Man of the Year as the top closer in the game. Then he was given the National League Cy Young Award as the best pitcher in the game — period. He is the first reliever to win since Dennis Eckersly of the Oakland Athletics in 1992.

50

Perdita Felicien
Hurdler

———∞———

Hometown: Pickering, Ontario

HURDLERS CAN'T GET TOO FAR AHEAD OF THEMSELVES. Their race requires world-class speed for the foot-race portion of the competition and technical mastery to get over the hurdles smoothly. The only thing a hurdler can focus on is "next." Next hurdle, next step. It takes years to master and most hurdlers break onto the world stage in their mid- to late-twenties. At least that's the way it was until Perdita came along.

Perdita was born in Oshawa on August 29, 1980. She grew up in Pickering and went to Glengrove Public School. She was the fastest kid on the track team, but she hated the hurdles even though she could fly over them. Then in high school, at Pine Ridge Secondary, when she was in grade 11 the track coach, Curt Sahadath, talked her into taking the hurdles seriously.

Perdita took her share of tumbles and had some dandy shin bruises while learning the basics of hurdling, but her confidence never shattered. When Donovan Bailey led Canada's track team to glory at the 1996 Atlanta Olympic Games, the high school hurdler in Pickering became inspired.

By 1997 Perdita was the best 100-metre hurdler in Ontario. By 1998 she was the best junior in the country. By 1999 she was on the national team and was offered a full scholarship to the University of Illinois. Coach Gary Winckler's program at Illinois is one of the best in the NCAA (National Collegiate Athletic Association) — especially for hurdlers. Perdita fit right in.

Her freshman NCAA season was silk. Perdita became a two-time All American by finishing in the top six nationally in the 100-metre hurdles and in the 400-metre relay with her teammates. In mid-April, during NCAA qualifications, she ran a 12.91-second 100-metre hurdles race — the second fastest in Canadian history. She was still just 19 years old.

That fall Perdita started school late with her school's and her coach's blessing, so that she could travel to Sydney and compete as a member of Canada's Olympic team. In Sydney Perdita failed to advance out of her first heat, but she saw the big Olympic show and practised alongside the best in the world. Coach Winckler reminded her that almost everyone has a bad first Olympics. At her age she'd have plenty more chances. Her confidence grew.

In 2001 she became Illinois Female Athlete of the Year. She won All-American honours in both the 100- and 60-metre hurdles and the U.S. Track Coaches Association selected her as the National Outdoor Athlete of the Year. At the 2001 World Championships, wearing the Canadian track-team's uniform, she got through her heat and into the semifinals. Although she didn't get to the finals, this was a huge improvement over Sydney. Perdita focused on next.

The 2002 season saw Perdita become an NCAA champion and a legend at her school. She won all but one race through the entire outdoor season while claiming victory in both the National Championship 100- and 60-metre hurdle races. Indoors, she was undefeated all season and set a new NCAA record of 7.90 seconds over 60 metres. She was ranked Number One right through the year. The NCAA knew Perdita was a star, but to the rest of the world she was a complete surprise package, one they'd see opened in 2003.

The indoor season in 2003 wasn't any indication of what lay ahead in the summer for Perdita. Her times were solid, her performances good, but her goals were to improve her starts and to keep up her grades. By the time the outdoor season rolled around, she was on form. She won the NCAA National Championship in 12.88 seconds. For fun she raced in a straight 100-metre contest at the Big Ten Championships and finished with an 11.78. Fast.

At the Pan Am Games in the Dominican Republic on August 9, Perdita lined up for the final of the 100-metre hurdles against some of the best in the sport. She ran a 12.70 and placed second to Brigitte Foster of Jamaica. The race proved to her that she could compete with anybody — even world champion Gail Devers of the USA, who'd missed the Pan Ams.

At practice, coach Winckler walked by and casually told Perdita that she could finish top three in the world. She thought about it. Then she started to believe. Next.

On August 27, 2003, Perdita walked into the light at Le Stade de France in Paris for the final of the 100-metre hurdles. Reigning champion Devers didn't get through to the final, but the field was deep. Brigitte Foster made it through; so did Jenny Adams of the USA. It was two days before Perdita's 23rd birthday. She was stoked.

In 12.53 seconds, in front of 60,000 screaming fans, Perdita became the champion of the world — the first Canadian win at the big meet since the men's 4 × 100 relay team took the title in 1997. Perdita was walking on the same ground as her heroes Donovan Bailey, Bruny Surin and Glenroy Gilbert. She was the first Canadian woman to ever win at the World Track and Field Championships. She was also the first Canadian woman to win on such a grand stage since the 1928 Amsterdam Olympics 4 × 100-metre relay team won gold. In 12.53 seconds Perdita had written history. She was on a cloud.

The first thing Perdita wanted after that win was some of her mom's cooking, so she came home to Canada and a backyard barbecue in Pickering. It was a feast of oxtail and tamarind balls, recipes her mom brought from St. Lucia.

Felicien's hometown threw a party, the mayor gave her the key to the city, she won the Bobbie Rosenfeld Award as Canada's Female Athlete of the Year, and Perdita had some decisions to make. For management, she turned to the great American hurdler and one-time San Francisco 49er wide receiver Renaldo Nehemiah. They negotiated a contract with Nike that would allow her to focus exclusively on the Athens Olympics in 2004. She wouldn't have to worry about rent or groceries anymore. Nehemiah called her the freshest breath of air to hit the track world in along time.

On March 6, 2004, at the World Indoor Championships in Budapest, Hungary, Perdita clocked 7.75 seconds in the 60-metre hurdles to break the championship record and her own Canadian national record.

Her mom's proudest achievement so far is Perdita's high academic college score. Next.